MAKING
CREATIVITY
ACCOUNTABLE

MAKING
CREATIVITY
ACCOUNTABLE

How Successful Advertisers Manage Their Television and Print

RON HARDING

QUORUM BOOKS

New York • Westport, Connecticut • London

Library of Congress Cataloging-in-Publication Data

Harding, Ron.
   Making creativity accountable :
how successful advertisers manage
their television and print
     p. cm.
   Includes index.
   ISBN 0–89930–337–4 (lib. bdg. : alk. paper)
    1. Television advertising—United States—Cost control.
   2. Advertising layout and typography—Cost control. I. Title.
HF6146.T42H336 1991
659.1′068′1—dc20   91–8651

British Library Cataloguing in Publication Data is available.

Library of Congress Catalog Card Number: 91–8651
ISBN: 0–89930–337–4

First published in 1991

Quorum Books, 88 Post Road West, Westport, CT 06881
An imprint of Greenwood Publishing Group, Inc.

Printed in the United States of America

The paper used in this book complies with the
Permanent Paper Standard issued by the National
Information Standards Organization (Z39.48–1984).

10 9 8 7 6 5 4 3 2 1

This book is dedicated to the memory of my father,
Charles Edward Harding,
one of America's great salesmen

Contents

Preface

Comedian Jay Leno on "The Tonight Show" observed: "What do you make of these new commercials? Boy! The other night I saw one for Infinity and then one for Levi's Cotton Dockers. Not only didn't I know what they were talking about, I got so confused I didn't even know who I was!"

Mr. Leno's identity crisis is shared by many advertisers. There is abroad in the land an advertising mind set that believes consumers don't want to be sold anything. Inside this logic pattern, the advertiser has been persuaded to mute his reason for being and to attempt assimilating consumers by understatement and misdirection.

In its role as apologist, advertising has changed direction, purpose and content. Advertising moves away from ideas to images, from competitive claims to a murmur of commonality. The viewer is not persuaded but lulled in a warm bath of connotation.

Redundant images emerge in commercial after commercial irregardless of what is being sold: naked father holding baby, farmer wiping sweat from brow, young woman fisting air in triumph, sax player tootling before hot neon background, petulant blonde leaning against car fender, couple snuggling in doorway, old couple dancing, family crowded around table in Norman Rockwell's living room, ballet dancers leaping, skylines, traffic, sunsets, waves, fields of grain.

Michelob Light with a media budget estimated to be upwards of $250 million truly monopolized the air for a year with a dazzling array of celebrities, original music and cutting edge production value. When the campaign wound down, Anheuser-Busch made the admission that no real sales headway had been made. Beer drinkers had no idea why Michelob Light came to market and had difficulty in even remembering they had seen the advertising.

Advertising as non-advertising, in short, has succeeded. But to what end? There is, of course, a presumption at work here. The advertiser who can afford to spend more and say nothing deserves audience reward and some sort of earned allegiance. In a way, this is very much like the mentality connected with the old Potlatch ceremonies practiced by the Indians of the Pacific Northwest. Potlatch is an ornate burning ritual where each village family drags out as much of its substance as it can afford to lose and tosses it into the conflagration. The group that can burn the most without suffering hardship is recognized to be village chief. Homage is paid. Super Bowl Sunday appears to be our National Potlatch Day, an electronic bonfire of the vanities determining some sort of marketing pecking order.

At issue then is advertising's basic premise. What is its purpose? Is it an end unto itself or the means to an end? For those advertisers without money to burn, this is the central question to be asked of the agency but ultimately answered by the advertiser himself.

Acknowledgments

A great many people have been responsible for my success in the advertising business; they number in the hundreds. A few individuals and companies must be singled out for special mention. First is Charles Claggett of Gardner Advertising, who hired me simply because I could remember the lyrics to a commercial I found especially memorable—and he had written. Harry Hill and Noel Digby were given the exhausting task of teaching me how to write copy and produce it.

At Procter & Gamble, sometimes called the Advertising School of Higher Learning, I was instructed by a host of professors, among them Gib Carey, Andy DeMar, Norm Levy and Miner Raymond. P&G's "copy college" is the source for most of my remarks in this book on the subjects of copy development and appraisal, managing copy meetings and the like.

Much of what I learned about production management was supplied by James Cochran. Many top managers have emerged from P&G thanks to his instruction and quiet example.

My ability to work with people in the creative area, as both a contributor and a supervisor, was learned from Dirk Wales, who has remained a good friend and advisor for more than twenty-five years.

At Gillette, where I inaugurated a new department and was able to put into practice many new creative and cost disciplines, a large measure of the credit is due to Tom Ryan, vice president of Advertising Services, and Bill Ryan, president of the Personal Care Division.

My staff—Jack Walp, June Zeiner, Steve Rapson and Judi Gecawicz—
played a significant part in developing and implementing many of the
systems and forms displayed in this book.

Valuable insights into agency patterns of copy and production were
provided by Allen Rosenshine and Karl Fischer at BBDO, New York.

I have so many friends at agencies and production companies in
New York City, Chicago and Los Angeles that it is impossible to
single out any individuals without slighting many more. I appreciate
their craftsmenship as well as fellowship over the years. I hope they
will recognize some of their insights and good humor in the following
pages.

I appreciate the help of Morty Dubin of the Association of Independent Commercial Producers (AICP) and Dennis Hayes of the
Association of Independent Commercial Editors (AICE) for furnishing
forms used in this book as well as the glossary of terms in Appendix
D. I appreciate as well the help of the Association of National Advertisers (ANA), DeWitt Helm's good offices and Dorothy Forget of
the American Association of Advertising Agencies (4A's) Broadcast
Committee for supplying me with various reports and tables and the
permission to quote from these sources.

Finally, I must make mention of the patience and quiet endurance
of my wife, Jean, and my editor, Eric Valentine, during the several
years it took for me to write and rewrite this book.

Introduction

The purpose of *Making Creativity Accountable* is to help you, the advertiser, manage your agencies and your own efforts in achieving great advertising at sound and predictable levels of spending.

This book is designed to show you how to rethink and possibly restructure the way you go about the business of creating, approving, producing and funding your advertising and the internal structure of your operating divisions. You may wish to consider this book simply as a means by which you can lower your production costs. What is being offered, however, is considerably more: It is a sophisticated approach to give your agencies more latitude to generate great work and assume greater accountability for their efforts. Great advertising ideas produce their own economies in production and media expenditures. This is no pie in the sky claim. Most advertisers who have used my systems report a genuine improvement in creative testing and a genuine dollar savings in all areas of advertising expense: production, talent and media. These are substantial savings, running into the millions of dollars.

As you probably know from your own experience in marketing, costs are nothing more than the result of what you build into design, the level of quality you demand and the time given over to manufacture. Whether all that pays out depends on how much you sell.

National television advertising is some forty years along in terms of experience and lessons learned. It would seem that most of the answers to the questions by now are self-evident. Selling by means of the home screen is nothing more than what selling has always been: telling prospective customers why your product is better than the competition's and why they ought to buy it.

What is remarkable is that every few years, advertisers and their agencies feel impelled to reinvent the wheel, yet the learning curve stays essentially flat. Why? Advertising depends on its vitality for newness, and this is largely accomplished by young people coming into the business. Youth is long on energy but short on experience. This need not be a problem as long as education and sufficient insulation is provided to these young people until their skill levels match their energy. Too often, this is not the case. Training programs are costly, and holding bodies in reserve until they come up to speed somehow seems inefficient and non-productive in today's bottom-line universe. Training programs are being slashed and new managers are being brought on-line faster.

Similarly, agencies and manufacturers have been downsizing in the name of productivity. First to go inside many companies are market research, R&D and advertising staff support groups—in short, anybody who is not directly involved in marketing and sales. Inside the agencies, where "creativity is our most important product," any department not directly involved in the creative process is being downsized. Market research, seasoned producers and senior account groups are in this group. The combination of the untrained agency creative coupled with the inexperienced brand manager can be a volatile combination.

The brand management system was never intended to be an advertising franchise. Creative intuition and marketing skills are distinct and separate disciplines. Good advertising depends heavily on risk taking. Good brand management depends on risk avoidance.

The combination of inadequate staffing, inadequate training and the wrong match of manager and need sets in place an atmosphere of mutual compliance and mutual distrust. The agency has always depended on the client to exercise management control. Without it, the agency is left to its own devices, a situation recalling Richard Rowland's comment about the Hollywood studios years ago when the creatives took over management ranks. "My God," said Rowland, an executive at MGM, "the inmates have taken over the asylum."

Advertising has always made the most expensive use of film, with the possible exception of NASA taking snapshots on the moon. Production in the advertising mode generates massive startup costs that cannot be defrayed in the same way movies and television make use and reuse of sets, costumes, sound stages and equipment. The advertiser has no means of amortizing costs over time. The advertiser also is using film in a way unique to advertising—working within expectation levels that demand split-second timing and working with a substantial amount of close detail on inanimate objects to give them an inherent value or worth often suggestive in nature. All this gives rise to an enormous amount of subjective judgment. Stanley Kubrick, no stranger to film or perfectionism, came away from a commercial shooting saying: "If features were shot that way, no one could afford to make them." It took Mike Cimino and *Heaven's Gate* to put a dollar dimension to Kubrick's observation.

Advertising costs have greatly accelerated since the start of the 1980s. This is not the result of advertising, per se, but rather the result of marketers who have dismissed their R&D groups and now have nothing much to bring to the marketplace but parity products and flanker brands. This puts the onus on advertising and agencies to artificially imply something of value. If the product is not worth talking about, agencies will attempt to suggest worth with their time-honored tradition of problem solving: throwing money at it until it goes away!

There is, however, a limit even to advertiser dollars. Cutting back on advertising and media (as well as staff support groups who used to bring expertise to the buying of both), advertisers now disappear from the airwaves for substantial periods of time. When they come back, they seek to make up for lost time by rolling out some outsized advertising—what has come to be called event advertising. This advertising may depart from what the advertiser has been running in the past simply because he has changed agencies or decided to reposition a brand slightly or brand managers have moved around inside the company and the new manager wants to put her stamp on the advertising. The result is that what the brand stands for—its character and continuity—is often lost in the shuffle. When the new advertising meets with little success in testing or the marketplace, yet another campaign is crash produced and aired. Frankly, more damage is done by marketers' changing their agencies and shifting advertising emphasis than their competition could ever hope to accomplish.

Not only shifts within companies but shifts among companies have had significant impact on how advertising is originated and what it is meant to do. Mergers and management mobility at every level have diminished much company character and company similitude. Be tween one operating division and the next, the only basis of commonality may be the name on the company letterhead.

The agency, let us not forget, is a service organization. That means it seeks to satisfy the client based on what the client says he or she wants, needs and is willing to pay. When no such advice is given to the agency, the agency is left to its own devices. These may or may not be in the company's and brand's best interests.

Clearly when no mention of costs is made, agencies and production companies operate as they always have, with a "whatever the traffic will bear" mentality. Said simply, if money is no object, no objections are anticipated about what is to be spent.

This is consistent with what agencies themselves say. Quite a number of agency CEOs have put the onus squarely on the advertiser. Allen Rosenshine at BBDO, for instance, has said simply: "Unless pressure is exerted on costs, upfront by the client, nothing much is going to happen." This means that the agency can and will design advertising to be successful within dollar frames providing the client provides these frames and works to help achieve them.

The company and its individual brand groups must have objective standards and some concentric means of working with the agency in a consistent, businesslike manner. Thus, although independent operating divisions may work in a highly autonomous manner, there must be some overriding pattern or system overlaid on the division that generates predictability for the agency.

The best-managed companies always provide clear operating disciplines for themselves and their agencies. They set up internal mechanisms to stay slightly ahead of the agency throughout the year in setting time frames, standards and goals. This is done in full knowledge of the fact that whoever leads the process controls it.

Most successful marketers-advertisers hold their agencies in high regard and work toward developing long-term relationships and a conducive, creative climate in which the agency can function and indeed risk presenting advertising that at first blush seems to take unnecessary chances. In reality, most successful advertising follows highly predictable givens in its creation, production and level of expense. The knowledgeable client thus provides creative freedom but exacts professional standards by a recognition of these givens.

Cost management is really nothing more than an outgrowth of the creative process and how well it is managed. Waste is merely buying more than is needed because clear articulation does not exist in advance on what is wanted. Waste also occurs in shooting elements that do not end up in the finished advertising. That waste exists in the commercial production area may be understood by the fact that most agencies expose 5,000 feet of film at every shooting to end up with 45 feet of film that makes up the finished thirty-second commercial.

Most successful advertisers know, sometimes intuitively, that the stronger the selling idea itself is, the less needs to be spent in producing either television or print. One of the most successful commercials of all time was created for Volkswagen. The commercial posed the simple question: "How does the man who drives the snowplow get to the snowplow?" The dramatic premise is so strong that production demands becomes secondary. The commercial is beautifully shot, directed and edited. But no comment has ever been made about the commercial's production values. The commercial is shot in a simple way because the idea requires no more. This is precisely the basis on which all great advertising operates and how it generates its own cost control.

I spoke to this basic understanding at a gathering of advertisers and agencies at the Plaza Hotel in New York City in 1981. My remarks (reproduced as Appendix E) that costs should be of secondary importance to the advertiser and the agency but are controlled by the creative process itself and early client instruction brought a good deal of attention to that premise, as well as to the success of the company for which I was then working, the Gillette Company. Gillette had staged a remarkable turnaround in its advertising and marketing fortunes. My contribution to this success was a matter of industry knowledge and public record.

The fact that Gillette had managed to shed its reputation as a "blue-collar advertiser" and was having substantial success in introducing new products and positioning them at premium prices provided ample testimony on the successful changes in Gillette's management systems in advertising. Not only was Gillette putting forth better advertising, its costs were stabilized and its scrapping rates of full-finished advertising (somewhere around 30 percent when I joined the company) had dropped to zero. Moreover, Gillette's agencies were enthusiastic about the new creative climate and were inviting me to talk with their other clients on how to put in place advertising systems they could use to simulate Gillette's progress. The systems, procedures, forms and ideas offered to Gillette and other advertisers and outlined in my speech are the basis for this book.

These systems are not my own invention. They have been patterned on forms, schedules and procedures used by many agencies in managing their own internal affairs. I attribute at least some of their success to the fact that agencies recognize how complementary these procedures are to their own needs and demands and internal workings.

I strongly believe in agencies and their inherent competence and honesty. I also strongly believe that advertising works and produces genuine sales results and profitability. Gillette in 1990 was able to cut its introductory spending levels for its new Sensor Razor by about 40 percent, thanks to the success of the campaign and the fact that demand was far outrunning supply. All manufacturers should have such problems!

Gillette is still using the systems I put in place on copy and advertising development, production and costs procedures, to its considerable advantage. Although I am associated with Gillette now only on a free-lance creative basis, I take some justifiable pride in its ongoing marketing success.

I am pleased to offer in this book the results of twenty-five years of experience in working with major advertisers and their agencies and the successful accomplishment of some 3,000 television commercials and print ads. The systems work. They will help you generate great advertising ideas, and those ideas will generate real savings in the production area. I wish you and your agencies much success in the years ahead.

MAKING
CREATIVITY
ACCOUNTABLE

1

Clarifying Advertising Purpose and Costs

What is advertising intended to do? The answer to this simple question largely defines how you as a company operate and the value you put on advertising. Obviously any examination of advertising and its costs is an examination of value and value systems.

Advertising as it is defined inside most successful companies is the sharing of information about a specific product in the most dramatic, compelling, persuasive and memorable fashion possible to generate sales for the brand and company and to provide increased profitability for the brand and company.

Marketing at its core is the examination of consumer needs and expectations and bringing to the marketplace a product that in some way fills those needs and expectations in a manner superior to that which currently exists. New products are introduced with some specific purpose in mind: to fill a need better, more completely, less expensively. Advertising is simply getting the word out to the consumer that such a product has arrived.

Most successful advertising is built on a copy strategy that articulates the marketing strategy and simplifies and focuses it. There may be many reasons that a particular product is superior to its competition, but the copy strategy seeks to articulate that advantage in a particularly simple and single-minded fashion. The copy strategy is a long-term entity that does not change unless the product itself has been reformulated or there is some significant change in the marketing environment or competitive situation.

The copy strategy provides both the client and the agency with a common basis for evaluating and discussing the merits of advertising submissions. Importantly, it saves a good deal of time because it eliminates the need to reinvent the wheel. Basic decisions do not need to be reviewed and rethought every time new advertising is considered for production.

The characteristics of a good copy strategy and, by extension, good advertising are clarity, simplicity, absence of unnecessary executional detail and inherent competitiveness. Good advertising is recognized by a single-minded reiteration of product benefit, essentially a literal expression of the product's functional purpose and a people benefit, a psychological or motivational reward that consumers may realize by purchase of the product.

Strategic positioning in most product categories has become increasingly difficult by brand proliferation, market fragmentation, increased commercial clutter and by management shifts, brand managers moving from brand to brand, division management changes caused by mergers and restructurings and the drop in skill levels caused by reduction in qualified senior managers and a lack of sufficient training on the client side as well as within agency ranks.

Over time, the purpose of advertising inside many companies has become diffused, as well as the means of best accomplishing the advertising. This is particularly true with companies where divisions tend to act more or less autonomously and where a commonality of purpose and an organizational matrix have become diffused as well. There is no question that centrist companies tend to act more homogeneously and share commonality in goals, purposes and systems. These companies are easier to work with because they are highly accessible to agencies and other suppliers. Centrist companies also tend to promote from within, put value in training and seek to promote longevity internally and with agencies and suppliers externally.

Continuity, predictability, shared systems and commonality of purpose are the hallmarks of companies that manage the advertising process most successfully and whose brands evidence longer life cycles and more consistent advertising campaigns. Advertising campaigns stretch over decades, and levels of profitability remain constant. Additionally, products begin to build character and establish marketing niches that are virtually unassailable by competition.

Because advertising is imminently predictable in what is looked for and what is required, costs are equally predictable. Advertising is reviewed on the basis of idea content, and production is simply an extension of necessary expenditures consistent with the brand's target audience and their levels of expectation. The further one moves from these standards of continuity, predictability, shared systems and commonality of purpose, the greater risks arise as to client control and agency supervision.

The role of the agency is a simple one: to make product benefit stories accessible and memorable to consumers. Agencies are limited by product performance furnished by the marketer as well as by available funds furnished by the marketer-advertiser. These limits are necessarily reductive in nature. But they also provide guidelines, focus and parameters by which the agency can judge its own performance.

Procter & Gamble is generally recognized as one of the world's most skilled and successful marketers. It is a classic example of the centrist organization. P&G is generally credited with having invented the brand management system, and it is worth examining how that system operates.

Brand managers are the lowest common denominator in the marketing system. Their decision making and authority are proscribed by their level of experience and the basic skills consistent with the MBA training learned at universities. At Procter & Gamble, an MBA degree is recognized as the admission fee to the world of marketing. A training period of two to five years is now put against every new brand manager; all are insulated from direct decision making not only in marketing but in advertising and production as well.

It is of critical importance for other companies that espouse the brand management system to realize that Procter & Gamble never intended marketing or brand managers to be actively involved in the creation or production of advertising. Through experience, P&G discovered that advertising and production skills are separate and unique skills that are as much intuitive processes as they are capable of instruction. Consequently P&G has not sought to grow advertising and production expertise in-house but rather to hire it from agencies and production houses outside and to turn responsibility over to these experts in the appraisal, guidance and funding of advertising and advertising production. Only when work is relatively far along and final options are to be selected does the brand manager begin to exert any real control.

The brand management system as it exists and is successfully implemented inside Procter & Gamble has rarely been replicated outside this company. Instead, many companies have attempted to make marketing managers into advertising managers and to turn back responsibility to product managers in controlling, supervising and directing agency activities in creation, production and funding of advertising. This is especially true in companies that retain minimal staffing and are division autonomous.

Advertising managers—vice presidents of advertising—inside many company divisions are marketing managers who have not made the final cut in inclusion into senior marketing ranks. The results of this decision, a salutory gesture on the part of management, are nearly always disastrous. As a senior manager at Procter & Gamble has put it: "It's like trying to turn a Clydesdale into a race horse."

Companies that have placed their advertising fortunes in the hands of managers who are intellectually disoriented in the advertising process show surprisingly similar results. Advertising budgets are poorly administered. Successful advertising campaigns are short-lived. Product life cycles show shortened longevity. Agency relations are short term and marked by agency frustration.

Lack of continuity, lack of successful advertising, a poor creative climate and out-of-control costs are the hallmarks of divisions managed without appropriate advertising leadership, disciplines and systems. Such divisions are largely inaccessible to change and problems to resolution as long as these managers are retained in positions of authority. Traditionally, companies that provide considerable division autonomy have generated fiefdoms whose operations are largely controlled by these advertising managers and who see the implementation of any companywide systems as an intrusion and imposition.

Staff support groups or advertising consultants make little or no headway in improving creative climate or promulgating management systems. By division mandate and usually with corporate agreement, such professionals are restricted to technical areas associated with advertising.

Realistically, all decisions that determine advertising success and costs are creative decisions made long before advertising moves into the bidding and production process. Unsuccessful advertising is flawed from its inception and has already built in its own waste. To attempt to provide remedy by technical means and last-minute cost cutting is an admission that the situation is already out of control and predetermined to fail.

What is overproduction? It is spending more money than is needed to tell the product story and make the sale. Where does overspending begin? Basically it grows out of a suspicion that telling a simple story will not interest or intrigue the audience. Audiences have been subjected to, or spoiled with, a surplus of riches over the past forty years by movies, television and commercials.

I should be clear, however, on what advertising is and is not. Advertising is not in competition with movies or television programs. Commercials may be entertaining, but they are not considered another entertainment source by the audience. Advertising is more akin to news—information structured to lead viewers through a thicket of available products and services and convincing them to buy one product in preference to all similar others.

Volumes have been written on why and how advertising works. All of them say essentially the same thing: The key to advertising success is the persuasive advancement of information based on the single-minded differentiation of one product from another. Clearly this is a function of idea content, not production content.

Everything we know about successful marketing and advertising is based on product differentiation—specifically, product performance based on the recognition of a specific need and outperforming competition in satisfying that need. Positioning—that all-important word in advertiser and agency thinking—is nothing more than a better selective matchup of target audience and product capability. Brand differentiation always has been, is still and probably always will be the key to successful advertising. Accomplishing this is a function of copy design, not production expense.

Everything we know about successful marketing and advertising is predicated on a single selling claim, the headline idea, the reason why. This single-minded reiteration of need, product, product performance and end result benefit is the basis of marketing and copy strategy. A single-minded copy strategy clears away subordinate claims, secondary promises or clutter. Successful commercial executions exhibit the same qualities: simplicity, directness, clarity. It should not surprise you, then, to discover that the most cost-effective advertising is also based on the same principles.

Overproduction may be understood to be the introduction of secondary elements—the inclusion of detail and other elements subordinate to the selling idea. How do these elements find their way into creative concepts and production? First and foremost is the confusion as to advertising's purpose: information. In a very real way, both advertisers and agencies are often too close to the process. Living day to day with their brands, they tire of reiteration, simplicity and directness because it seems so commonplace and ordinary. They assume that audiences do as well. Wearout is as much a function of the advertiser-agency mentality as it is a true reading of audience perception.

Don't forget that viewers are bombarded with hundreds of messages each day on television, in newspapers and magazines, on radio and on billboards and in the mailbox. Most of it is forgotten or tossed away because the viewer is not ready to make a buying decision in a particular area at that time. You know through your own experience that diaper commercials hold absolutely no interest for you until you have a baby. Then absorbency, comfort, size, fit and adhesive tabs take on a world of meaning. None of this may be fascinating information, but it is suddenly useful information.

Viewers seek out advertising in a selective manner. Once they have tuned you in because of a particular need, the opportunity is now yours to tell your advertising story. (This is one reason advertising recall tests reflect overall low interest and advertisers are led to believe only some "borrowed interest" will help boost memorability.)

Successful advertising depends on selectivity—positioning of the product. What is most important? In television, you have fifteen or thirty seconds to tell your product story. In print, you have a quarter page, half page, page or double-page spread to do the same. How much picture? How much copy? What picture? What words? The integration of words and pictures, in television and in print, is crucial. So is the proper selection of words and pictures. Finding a single selling idea that persuades customers that you have predicted and satisfied their needs is at the heart of good marketing and good advertising.

"Less is more" is the key to success. Exclusion is as important as inclusion. Once the selling idea is parsed down to a single-minded sale, this information may then be given to consumers in a number of ways—television, radio, print—and in a variety of moods—serious, humorous, fanciful, emotional. Any number of successful executions may be generated at any number of cost levels once the selling idea is clear in the advertiser's and the agency's mind.

Remember the process that got you to the point of advertising: You discovered a consumer need and invented a product to fill that need. You gave greatest importance to some particular aspect in developing the product: better performance, better service, better packaging, better price. That is your reason for being; that is your marketing strategy. Your copy strategy was developed to summarize and make clear your marketing premise. Now you have before you a piece of advertising that is designed to dramatize and make clear your product story. What are the first things you as a marketer should look for?

1. Is this storyboard telling my product story?
2. Is my product the hero of this storyboard?
3. Does this advertising specifically show and dramatically explain why my product was brought to market?
4. Will the viewer understand why my product is better and delivers something the others don't?
5. If I didn't know anything about this product before, would this make me want to run out and buy it?

This is really all you are asking your advertising and agency to do, so extend this logic and make it actionable. Take a pen or pencil, and strike out every frame in the storyboard that is not working to set up your story and lead you to the product difference. Strike out every sentence or word that does not lead to the selling idea. Circle areas where words and pictures do not reinforce each other, and see if they can be moved to join forces. What you are doing here is taking a giant step forward in simplifying and strengthening your advertising. What you are also doing is isolating and removing production elements that eventually will lead to overproduction, overspending and wasted dollars. Those elements will be removed at the storyboard stage or edited out of the final commercial. What is edited out at the storyboard stage does not have to be bought and then thrown away.

Who knows the product better than you? Copy is only an extension of the marketing process, and production is only an extension of the copy process. There is, there must be, a straight line of action at work

that is clear, uncluttered and discernible: marketing to copy to production, clean and simple. Depend on your own good marketing
instincts. They are what helped you spot the marketing opportunity
in the first place.

2

Developing a Creativity-Cost Equation

The press of business keeps every brand, division and company focused on the future. Generally overlooked for that reason is the wealth of information already available—information that can help you assess future advertising success and costs with a high degree of predictability.

You have in hand, or should have, past scores associated with submitted advertising and costs associated with that advertising in production, talent and media expenditures. It is unlikely you have attempted to use this information to correlate actual success rates of advertising along with costs and results in terms of sales effectiveness and profitability. That is what we are about to do.

"Advertising is an art, not a science" usually describes the mindset surrounding the credibility of investigating the effectiveness of advertising dollars. Actually advertising is neither an art nor a science; it is a craft. As such, certain designs may be recognized to be more successful than others, and certain guidelines may be extracted from past performance to ensure a better chance for probable success in the future.

Your company undoubtedly makes use of some testing system in assessing advertising worth: recall, persuasion, intention to buy and the like. These tests are used to help you sort out which individual commercials appear to have a chance of being better remembered, providing better product differentiation, promoting a more persuasive reason to generate consumer interest or something else. While I am sure both you and the agency agree that testing is something less than perfect, it still gives some measure of comparability and worth on which to make a creative decision.

Each commercial is unique in some areas; it is similar in others. It falls into a genre or format that may be identified: tabletop, presenter, vignette, song and dance and so forth. Each of these commercial types has its own strengths and weaknesses in terms of communication impact. Over time, an examination of various commercial types will reveal their inherent strengths and weaknesses. This is not to say that one commercial type may not be more skillfully written than another but rather to recognize the general communications' impact inherent in various commercial types. Voiceover commercials, for instance, nearly always show lower recall scores than commercials with direct voice. Commercials whose advertising message is importantly carried by music always tend to score lower in initial testing but may slowly build over time to achieve significant memorability. Commercials with a storyline—with a beginning, middle and end or at least a sense of closure—tend to be more clearly understood than mood or other forms of unstructured commercials. Some products and their stories seem naturally to be better explained and dramatized by one type of commercial rather than another. This linkage of communication necessity and commercial format may be substantiated on the basis of your brand, division and company experience over time.

An in-house research group or an advertising manager with legitimate copywriting credentials can spearhead this examination. If neither is on staff, consider retaining the services of an outside advertising consultant.

Your already produced and tested advertising should be re-examined as far back as you can go, say four years. This advertising should be assembled in terms of commercials that scored well above the norm, slightly above norm, at norm and below norm—in short, a best-to-worst communications continuum. Not only should these commercials be listed in descending order along with their test scores on paper, they should be assembled on a viewing reel and looked at in terms of communication takeaway to discover what most often works or does not. This review will help sharpen the skills of division managers.

Now assemble your commercials in terms of production costs on a brand-by-brand, division-by division and companywide basis. Split out full-finished advertising, test, radio, print and promotional advertising. This cost analysis will reveal that certain types of commercials carry with them a built-in level of expense due to their internal complexity. You will also find that certain agencies and certain creative groups within your agencies present certain commercial formats consistently—these formats demanding a certain dollar level to be successfully produced.

These creative groups and their advertising are not only inherently more expensive but are driving up the costs of all your advertising companywide. The reason is simple: Once one agency breaks the barrier of permissible costs for your company, all other agencies will present advertising that reaches this new dollar level.

In analyzing costs paid for production of television, print, radio and promotion, also keep a running total in costs of talent, post-production and the normal rate of increase charged to brands over and above the estimated cost of the advertising. Isolate as well the amount of scrapped full-finished advertising by brand, division and agency. If enough expertise exists, also factor in media spending against campaigns to generate a total advertising dollar outlay.

A word of caution belongs here: Keep all information gathering pure and analyses clean. Be aware that the greater refinement that is attempted, the greater is the skill level required by those surveying the data. Internal financial groups who often suggest themselves for this sort of analysis are rarely a good idea; they lack the background, training and knowledge of advertising and production. Attempting merely to analyze numbers without a quality frame of reference leads to surveys, findings and reports that may be seriously off the mark.

The final cost analysis should show costs reflected low to high in every category—full finished, test, print, radio, talent, media—and broken out by agency, division and brand—in short, a best-to-worst cost continuum.

You now have in hand creative results and costs organized to reflect effectiveness and expended dollars. By matching these numbers against each other, you will find some intersecting point where those commercials that scored highest were produced at the lowest costs. On a per brand, per division, per agency basis, you have arrived at your own favorable creativity-cost equation. This will provide you with a long-range forecasting and appraisal device for the future.

You may also wish to compare your costs with averages published each year by the American Association of Advertising Agencies (4A), which reflects costs by product category paid by national advertisers as revealed in a survey of some 2,141 commercials. These costs do not reflect agency commission. Following is the 4A's display for 1989:

Product Category	Cost
Automobiles/Trucks/Motorcycles	$235,000
Automobile Accessories/Supplies	$173,000
Beauty/Fashion/Cosmetics	$197,000
Gifts/Toys/Hobbies/Recreation	$146,000
Furniture/Appliances/AV Products	$133,000
Apparel & Clothing	$154,000
Banking/Financial/Insurance	$250,000
Consumer Services/Retail Stores	$231,000
Corporate Image/Media Promotion	$274,000
Travel/Vacation Destination	$242,000
Beer/Wine	$299,000
Soft Drinks/Snacks	$231,000
Retail & Fast Food Restaurants	$138,000
Packaged Food	$123,000
Household Products	$158,000
Drugs/Toiletries	$111,000
Office Equipment/Computers	$187,000

You may be surprised to learn as a result of your analysis that your most expensive commercials scored at or below the norm. You may be surprised to find the simplest, most modestly produced advertising was best remembered and most persuasive, perhaps because of that simplicity.

Of real significance here is the classifying together of costs and communication effectiveness. If sales and profitability results may also be compared to dollars spent in advertising, you have developed the larger outlines of true advertising value. This in turn may provide you with new information by which to assess agency and division managers. Certainly this review will put agencies and divisions on notice that new appraisal systems are in effect. This appraisal must play some part in future performance reviews and compensation. Not until that correlation is made will much be accomplished.

3

Enlisting Agency Support

The best time to meet with your agencies is when they are not actively working on a specific piece of copy or some production is in the works. Agencies tend to keep their eyes on the current target and may infer that your comments are not directed at overall efforts but are somehow related to work in progress. It seems practicable that some sort of review on advertising effectiveness and production efficiency should be held inside the agency at the beginning of the business year. This is an appropriate time and place to set before the agency a new business agenda and guidelines for the coming year.

Everyone associated with your advertising should be at this meeting: account, creative, production, business affairs, heads of departments. Position this review as a learning experience and an open discussion:

> We've been reviewing our advertising over the past several years from the standpoint of copy effectiveness and costs of production, and we've come up with some data that we found interesting and we hope you will find helpful. What we're going to do is to show you a reel of commercials that has been compiled in terms of most effective and least effective. What we mean by these terms is an attempted correlation between communication effectiveness and costs to produce. We've assembled them according to which commercials scored most effectively in terms of communication and whose costs were somewhere in the middle range of our production expenditures. What we would

like to do is to show you what we have found and then enlist your help in analyzing commercial content and costs. I'm passing out a piece of paper now that reflects communication scores and production costs for each commercial.

When the lights come up, sit back and let the agency talk. You will be surprised at the wide range of reactions inside each agency and between agencies. If experience is any guide, the agency touted as your most creative will express indignation that any sort of examination has taken place and that any measurement of effectiveness is being attempted. Your appropriate reaction is: "Of course, there is no perfect solution for judging commercial worth. But communication scores and costs taken together seem to be a valid way to begin appraising advertising. If this seems inappropriate, what would you suggest?"

Watch for some helpful input from the agency. Who is leading the discussion: account, creative, production? Whoever is taking the lead in discussion and seems to be generating the agency's position is undoubtedly the controlling partner in the agency's affairs.

Listen and take notes. It is the agency's business to know about advertising—presumably more about it than you know—so listen with genuine interest and openness. If the agency suggests, for instance, that sales results are the ultimate test of advertising effectiveness, perhaps recall scores should not play a part in your investigation. The agency may suggest that media weight be plowed into the factoring process. After all, the best commercial in the world will have no impact if it is not shown with proper reach and frequency. You should be attempting to foster agency input, agency leadership, agency congruity and a measurable, acceptable means of correlating advertising success and cost. Down the road should your company ever attempt to base agency compensation on agency performance, it will be most helpful to refer the agency back to its own suggested formula for realistic results-oriented measurement.

There are some other important discussion points to be raised in this meeting. If certain commercial types have clustered in the low range of communication effectiveness, ask the agency why. It may well be the vignette commercial with a number of different scenes piling atop one another. Vignette commercials are currently being used across all product lines, for introductory as well as ongoing advertising, to sell beers, cars, cosmetics, foods, insurance, office machines, soft drinks, telephone services, travel and so forth. They are among the most expensive commercial formats to shoot because of their quick jumps from set to set to location to location, all of which must be reached, propped, dressed, lighted and peopled with a vast number of principal players and extras. Such commercials also require longer editing and post-production schedules, nearly always use original music and are the most difficult to complete without extensive post-production. They are also frequently among the least coherent, least persuasive, least remembered commercial formats in the arsenal of agency firepower. Moreover, because so many advertisers are using vignette commercials, they tend to run together in consumers' minds and get lost in the nightly onslaught of commercials. Try to remember what you saw last night. Chances are it was that baby smiling out of the Kodak ad or the kitten playing with a box of cat food—advertising that was simple to shoot and memorable.

Understand that you are not trying to tell the agency what to create but to come to some understanding about what you and they perceive to be good advertising. If you have been seeing a good deal of vignette advertising submitted for consideration and have found it less than effective, it is certainly appropriate to say: "Given the high costs and rather fragmentary remembrance of vignette formats, should we realistically be looking at this as an option in the future?"

The subject of production quality should also come up at this discussion. Do any of your commercials stand out as being poorly produced advertising that reflects badly on the brand and company? If not, looking at a range in production costs of $150,000 to, say, $450,000 raises the important issue of how much more is being achieved by more ambitious production. Again, you are attempting to establish some commonality of purpose and value for the dollar. Advertising is only a selling vehicle to get you from here to there; that vehicle need not always be a Jaguar.

Where does the agency stand on testing? What has been happening in the area of test? Does the agency hold that certain commercial types cannot be tested? Why? Do these commercials always represent a substantial dollar investment and represent substantial risk of not communicating and ultimately being thrown away? How does the agency propose to get around this problem in the coming year?

Now that you have put the agency on record that results are being very carefully monitored, that costs and commercial effectiveness are being predicated as measures of advertising and agency value, it is time to open up the subject of procedural problems. Do you and the agency seem forever behind schedule and rushing to catch up? Why? Do you and the account group seem to agree on what creative next steps should be but never see this reflected in actual copy development? Why? Is there a lot of cross-talk between the company and agency with various groups making separate decisions about the same subject? Why?

Be specific about problem areas in communications, schedules, timetables, planning, costs and cost overruns. Ask the agency if this has anything to do with the way you and your division are working. Press them on this! The agency will always be hesitant to point out your shortcomings, you are the client, after all. Let them know you are expecting to see more uniform results in advertising quality and costs in the coming year, and if there is anything you are doing to impede that success, you want to hear about it now or in the near future when the agency has had the opportunity to discuss it among themselves.

You may be surprised to learn that many ongoing problems originate within client ranks. The agency is a service organization. Its staff tries to make the best of whatever is handed it. More likely than not, cross-talk, unrealistic timetables, lack of planning and runaway costs are all results of client work habits. Remember that the agency can only work up to the level of client competence.

The agency may not feel comfortable discussing this face to face. Ask them to put their thoughts in writing, holding the discussion to systems and policies as much as possible. Do the same in your own examination. Minimize focus on individuals. Chances are it is the position, not the person occupying the position that is the real cause of the problem. Remember that both you and the agency were hired on the basis of your proved competence. You are only attempting to build on that level of achievement.

Take time to caucus after meetings with everyone who attends from the client side. Assess what you have heard, what you believe was accomplished, where there are sure to be sticking points that need resolution and areas you and the agency have isolated for improvement. Establish a meeting time to pursue those areas and discover how your company can make its own efforts more realistic and efficient. Be sure you thank the agency staff for their time, patience, cooperation and insights.

Make sure the individuals and divisions who have initiated these discussions are singled out for recognition. They have already contributed significantly in helping to accomplish a better creative climate for the agency and establishing long-term quality and cost results for the company.

4

What Should a Commercial Cost?

In your examination of costs to date, you have undoubtedly discovered some important points. First, there is no right cost for a commercial. Second, there are a number of approaches to telling your product story—various executional formats that will all accomplish that end. Third, various commercial formats largely dictate their own costs, due to their internal complexity. Fourth, commercial complexity may actually be working against a clear focused exposition of your product story.

The question "What should a commercial cost?" frequently asked by advertisers is really open-ended—something like asking, "What should a car cost?" or "What should a house cost?" The only satisfactory answer to that question returns you to a value equation. "What is the purpose of advertising?" "What need do I place on any particular commercial to grow the business?" Commercial need in your year's advertising flow should determine what you spend at any point.

Clearly there are times when one particular commercial may appear to be more important to the brand. Introductory advertising or some product reformulation may be such an occasion. The words *new* and *improved* are probably the two most successful ones in the advertisers' lexicon to promote viewer attention and interest.

As long as your marketing and copy strategy remain the same, your advertising should remain the same—that is, your basic advertising thrust should remain consistent with only slight executional variances requested or permitted. Most successful brands thrive on continuity in advertising. This builds momentum and brand character and develops a marketing niche that is virtually unassailable by competitors. Continuity also promotes its own cost economies. When advertising becomes more predictable, so do its costs. You and the agency both know what to expect, and advertising is now subject to only fine tuning, not invention.

Continuity permits you to run advertising longer and shoot it in pools. Bunching production activity by shooting two or three commercials at a time reduces costs of each commercial by as much as 30 to 40 percent. Pooling commercials also takes the pressure off the production of any single piece of advertising. Psychologically, the concentration of effort on a single commercial tends to promote overindulgence and overimportance attached to this single effort. That leads to overproduction and "the elusive pursuit of the perfect :30."

Keep reminding yourself and the agency that your advertising is an ongoing effort, something akin to turning out a daily newspaper. If you keep your advertising in perspective, you will avoid the trap of putting all your eggs in one basket and creating a Fabergé egg in the process.

Consistency in advertising has other benefits. Consistent efforts permit you to run advertising longer. Commercials have a much greater life span than you may think. Remember that while you live with the same advertising day in and day out for years, your audience sees it only once or twice a week at most. Besides, they are bombarded with hundreds of commercials each day. It takes years before the audience is saturated with your brand's advertising. Look at the life span of successful campaigns like Procter & Gamble's stable of products: Bounty's "Quick Picker Upper," Cascade's "Sheeting Action," Downy's "Deep Downy Feeling," Folger's "Mountain-Grown Flavor," Joy's "See Yourself Shine," and what has proved to be the best-remembered advertising in the past twenty years as determined by an independent national survey, "Please Don't Squeeze the Charmin." (I take some pride here; I worked on three of these campaigns.) Other advertisers have discovered the same value in continuity, sometimes using continuing characters as product spokesmen: Charlie the Tuna, Palmolive's Madge the Manicurist, Dow's Scrubbing Bubbles, the Jolly Green Giant, the Maytag Repairman.

All of this advertising gains its vitality from reiteration and continuity and the promotion of a single selling idea. Moderate costs of producing this advertising are simply a by-product.

Ongoing advertising also permits the advertiser to reuse footage already shot in effective and memorable ways. Demonstrations and product signature shots may be used over and over again for years, focusing interest on a product's "reason why" and closing the sale with an encapsulation of the message in a single visual.

Focus, selection, reiteration: these are the hallmarks of great advertising. They are also the best cost controls you can hope to exert.

There are larger cost savings to be realized as well. Commercials that are used with longer running schedules eliminate the need to shoot more advertising. Commercials that run longer pay out with economies in talent reuse cycles. Commercial commonality also requires less media spending. Introductory advertising requires a heavy media schedule to register an impression. Ongoing advertising is reminder advertising and requires less frequent exposure. Brands may save millions of dollars each year in production, talent and media costs by the simple act of continuous reiteration of the same idea, and build sales more effectively in the process.

Your creative decision making—what advertising you choose to buy—is the single most important controlling element in dictating commercial costs. Commercial concepts carry their own price tags. You have witnessed this in your own examination of costs. Another proved indicator is the 4A's report displaying costs paid by national advertisers in 1989 on the basis of executional format selected by those advertisers. This report is worth examining carefully to remind you that the advertising the agency chooses to write and you choose to buy largely determines the costs you will pay to produce that advertising. These figures are gross costs before commission and displayed by commercial type:

Commercial Type	Average Cost
Interview/testimonial	$ 76,000
Tabletop/ECU products and food	$ 93,000
Monologue	$ 97,000
Animation	$156,000
Single situation: Dialogue	$174,000
Single situation: Product performance	$175,000
Single situation: Voice-over	$176,000
Multi-story line/vignettes	$228,000

Special effects	$263,000
Song and dance	$277,000

The notion that the creative group can write anything it wants and the brand group can buy whatever it likes and then arbitrarily attempt to dictate a cost ceiling has just been proved fallacious. Advertising can and must be written with a specific production cost in mind. Professionals can do this; amateurs won't.

5

Turning Knowledge into
Action: The Spending Plan

The purpose of an annual spending plan is to provide specific cost guidelines for the agency before the creative and production activity begins. These guidelines are set in place with the understanding that both the agency and the brand group will be unified in their efforts to develop and approve advertising consistent with these dollar limits. The spending plan shows *what* advertising is to be produced, *when*, *at what cost* and aired at *what level* of media spending. The spending plan is a working document and an indispensable cost control mechanism.

Given its importance, it is surprising the spending plan is so casually produced inside many companies and ignored by many others. One major cosmetic advertiser seeking assistance in managing television and print costs admitted to never committing his brands to a spending plan: "We never know what our agencies are going to come up with," the vice president of advertising says. Not surprisingly, his production, talent and media costs are staggeringly overpriced, creative levels are uneven and communication of even basic ideas is difficult to detect.

Many clients do not mention costs or cost ceilings to the agency with the admirable intent of not wanting to stifle creativity, but costs will eventually become an issue. Not telling the creative group at least the outside dollar limits that must be recognized is to do the agency a disservice, regardless of intent. This is somewhat analogous to telling the creatives their work need not be of any specific length or designed for any specific medium. By your withholding information the agency is working in the dark.

A clear, consistent, focused approach to the business of advertising is necessary for the agency to understand not only client costs but client purpose. Are print and television to carry identical messages? Or is print to be an information carrier and television an emotional hook? What balance is to be achieved? Defining advertising purpose for the agency prepares them to understand where dollars are to be shepherded and spent.

If your brand has limited funds, you will want to avoid any sort of image, special effects or song and dance advertising that is inherently expensive to shoot and air and instead come at your target audience with a more focused, clearly reasoned creative approach that is immediately accessible. Limited media weight almost certainly demands straightforward exposition to ensure that each exposure registers clearly and immediately.

At planning discussions with all elements of the agency, the client's objectives must be clearly stated and demonstrated in appropriate spending levels. Is current advertising ongoing next year, or will there be some creative shift? How much? How will this affect costs? In what area? Is there some major emphasis to be placed on advertising in the coming year: a product improvement, a flanker brand? Dollars must be set aside for that major push. Again, this may indicate that current advertising should be run longer, which will have an impact on talent and residual cycles or demand contract extensions. If celebrity talent figures importantly in upcoming advertising, time must be set aside for contract negotiations and a period of testing to see if the talent has sufficient drawing power to justify the dollar demands.

The spending plan defines agency and client purpose, puts a dollar figure against each category of expense and acts as a forecasting and month-by-month update of planned versus actual. Without planning, dramatic shifts may be forced on the brand to finance one element that has suddenly grown out of all proportion to the whole. On more than one occasion, I have seen advertising produced and then never aired because dollars could not be found to fund necessary talent and residual costs.

Because the spending plan is organized on a quarterly basis, it also serves as a self-actuating calendar of events to signal the initiation of creative activities. Starting the creative process on time eliminates the need for crash production schedules later.

Given the importance of this document, the spending plan should be prepared by the most knowledgeable participants available to the client: the advertising support group or an advertising-production consultant hired on retainer. The division is to be considered the conduit of information, marketing and advertising joining forces to articulate purpose and timetables. The account group is a source of information gathering and planning within the agency. Based on this accumulated knowledge, it is the responsibility of the division advertising manager or his or her assigned specialist to set realistic spending levels in every category of expense. Importantly, dollar reserves are identified to be held until the quarter when major activity is designed to happen: a brand relaunch, introduction of a flanker brand or something else. Dollar shortfalls are avoided in this manner.

Putting appropriate costs against every element, television, print, talent and media places a dollar ceiling on all activities, thus serving as a before-the-fact cost control mechanism. This in turn forces accountability in creating and producing advertising consistent with its importance in the year and pre-set spending levels.

On a quarterly basis or every month (as the client designates), the account group is expected to update all costs—actual-of-pocket dollars as well as dollars committed to work in progress. In this way, the account group and brand manager have a complete overview of events and their costs. Only moderate differences should be seen between planned versus actual. Dramatic shifts in major categories of expense should alert the client to some breakdown between account and other agency groups and will demand immediate attention.

Because the account group is the client's representative inside the agency and is expected to oversee and control timetables, activities and spending intelligently, the spending plan provides the account group with substantial leverage in accomplishing the client's goals. Thus, the spending plan forces accountability and responsibility in all agency departments and disciplines.

Let's look at a suggested spending plan format (see Exhibit 5.1). As you can see, the first page is devoted to costs associated with production. Page 2 reflects costs associated with talent use fees and mechanical costs, costs of duplicating quantity dubs of commercials. (The film category has virtually disappeared, but there are cases when film is still used—at sales meetings for instance, or when large crowds need focus on a screen larger than television size.) It is anticipated that the account group will submit a recap on all spending by the fifth of every month or on a quarterly basis, depending on client instruction.

The validity of the spending plan depends on fixed dollars.

Exhibit 5.1
Production Spending Plans Year

BRAND AGENCY OF RECORD	ACCRUED TO DATE	COMMITTED TO DATE	PLANNED	AVAILABLE FUNDS	MIDYEAR FORECAST	BUDGET
TV PRODUCTION (test/ff)						
1st Quarter						
2nd Quarter						
3rd Quarter						
4th Quarter						
Total TV Production:						
PRINT PRODUCTION						
1st Quarter						
2nd Quarter						
3rd Quarter						
4th Quarter						
Total Print Production:						
RADIO PRODUCTION						
1st Quarter						
2nd Quarter						
3rd Quarter						
4th Quarter						
Total Radio Production:						

OTHER PRODUCTION

1st Quarter
2nd Quarter
3rd Quarter
4th Quarter

Total Other Production:

TV/RADIO USE FEES (by commercial)
Commercial Name/#

Total:

PRINT TALENT FEES
Print Ad Title

Total:

FILM/TAPE
Yearly

Total:

MISCELLANEOUS
Yearly

Total:

TOTAL PRODUCTION SPENDING PLANS:

27

"Planned" is the category under which the particular cost of a commercial or print ad is indicated at the beginning of the year. "Committed to Date" reflects those dollars already allocated to be spent although not yet sent forward. (A production bid, for instance, reflects the total price, even though actual dollars may be sent forward on a proportional basis, fifty = forty = ten.) Because plans may change to some extent, the category "Midyear Forecast" reflects planning shifts away from original thinking. "Available Funds" reflects those dollars still accessible. To that end, divisions should do away with contingency funds—funds normally held in reserve and understood to be available to brands and agencies that express the need for additional dollars. If the money is there, it will most assuredly be needed and always by those who do the worst job of administering their own funds. Some divisions insist that such cushions and drains must be available in anticipation of some unexpected assault in the marketplace by a competitor. Such unexpected assaults generally indicate poor marketing prescience or a knee-jerk reaction to any unforeseen development. If your marketing niche is secure, your ongoing advertising should be strong enough to withstand any such incursion. If it is not, your marketing position, not your advertising, is usually at fault.

Contingencies built into agency agreements and bids should also be eliminated. Many agencies ask for a 10 percent contingency factor in television and print available to be spent with no formal notification or approval by the client. Such funds will always be spent, and then additional dollars will be requested in the form of overages. Begin now to discontinue the practice of contingencies wherever they may exist.

Corporate management also has a responsibility to both brand and agency not to raid brands in the third and fourth quarter of the year. This has become an all-too-frequent practice, with management arbitrarily scrapping production and media to drop those saved dollars to the bottom line and indicate greater profitability than actually exists. This may sometimes be necessary but should not be the annual scavenger hunt it has become. This merely encourages brands and agencies to spend aggressively in the first half of the year, regardless of advertising events and their importance.

The spending plan format I have supplied is a simple, effective document. It has been developed with the assistance of many different agencies and refined through client use. If your company has a similar document and it has been working, continue using it. There is no magic associated with any form.

Do not feel a need to complicate any forms. Usually the simpler the form is, the more wholeheartedly it will be endorsed and used. Try to bring uniformity to bear in whatever forms you use across all division lines and between agencies. Invite agency comment on all forms suggested here. Your agencies may have internal documents they are already using and may now be willing to share with you. These may be more sophisticated in nature but not necessarily better. Use whatever form seems to suit your purposes best, and make certain it is used companywide. Consistency makes use and reading of information more quickly accessible.

If you have a corporate logo or corporate color, you may wish to incorporate its use in printing your forms. This is a helpful reminder to your agencies that they are handling your plans and your dollars and their actions and results are being monitored by your forms.

Let's return to your agencies' track records as they relate to brand average, company averages, industry averages and your prediction of increases for the coming year. The advertising industry has reflected enormous increases since 1980 in both television and print. Costs of production have increased about 250 percent in that period and far outstripped the consumer price index, union increases, cost of materials and others. There has been little justification for these increases save for the usual whatever-the-traffic-will bear attitude so prevalent in the advertising community. Advertisers, agencies and production companies all shoulder some measure of responsibility for these increases.

Past performance should bear some relationship to future spending. The agencies that have done the best job of managing your funds should not be subjected to the same restrictions as those agencies that have proved cavalier in their spending. It would be wise for you to index appropriate percentage increases in spending based on prior agency performance. That is, agencies that are currently spending $100,000 per commercial should be allowed an increase of 12 percent next year. Those spending over $200,000 per commercial should receive an increase of no more than 7.5 percent. Any agency or brand group spending over $300,000 per thirty-second commercial should probably be frozen at that level of spending. Some clear signal must be sent to agencies and operating divisions that the ground rules have changed and that cost management is now being seriously enforced within your company.

Some clients are even proposing that agency commissions be factored against their operating costs, with commissions sliding downward in response to dollars spent. Other advertisers are examining paying their agencies a flat fee, with additional compensation based on some measurable performance factor, that is, above-average recall scores, meaningful attitude shifts in public awareness or some verifiable rise in sales. As long as this measurement is done fairly and consistently and agencies have some input into the measurement standards, these ideas reflect a solid, businesslike basis for agency remuneration. Equally, the same sort of performance measure needs to be put against division and brand management inside your company.

The agencies' first and most important points of contact throughout the year are division managers. If costs have been skyrocketing over the years and no serious efforts have been put against stopping them, the operating divisions have either been willing participants or ineffectual managers. Either way, their compensation and standing within the company should reflect those efforts (or their lack).

The agency takes its marching orders from the client. It also carefully monitors client management patterns. Company intent is understood by what you do, not what you say. When corporate management begins to exact firm standards of performance inside its operating divisions, the agency will be obliged to follow suit.

6

Controlling Time: The Project Initiation Form

Now that you have established clear-cut cost guidelines for the agency prior to the start of the year, the next important step in managing advertising and the advertising process is the proper management of time. Losing control of time puts the advertiser at a distinct disadvantage. He or she loses control of quality, costs and options and the full expertise the agency has to offer. It is not unusual to see cost increases of 50 to 200 percent occur in both television and print because work was begun too late. These additional dollars are not buying quality; they are buying time.

Every company will occasionally be faced with a crash production schedule and consider the premium paid an unfortunate but necessary expenditure. The company or division that finds itself habitually working under crash production schedules does not know how to budget its time or prefers the adrenaline rush and pressured environment artificially created. Hands-on managers are particularly susceptible to inventing crises that only they can now resolve. Crash production schedules should be recognized for what they are: the costly results of poor management practices inside client ranks and the loss of control of the advertising process inside the agency.

Where schedules most often become confused is in not linking copy development and production development and seeing them as a flow, with each requiring essentially the same amount of time. Although production cannot begin until the copy process is nearly completed, many clients assume that once copy is approved, the commercial or print ad will be delivered in short order. Some even think that if the agency is pushed through the production process, costs will somehow be lower because of reduced staff time.

Exactly the opposite is true, of course. For every week shaved off normal production schedules, a surcharge will be put atop usual costs. The client who demands advertising "next week" simply agrees to pay whatever surcharge is needed to accommodate this unrealistic schedule. By way of example, one soft drink manufacturer decided in mid-December to crash produce a commercial in time for Super Bowl Sunday. This gave the agency six weeks to create and produce the advertising. Originally estimated at $745,000, the commercial eventually came in at $1.5 million, and additional dollars (never announced) were spent in post-production fixing. The commercial was produced in such haste that neither the client nor the agency found it acceptable, and it never made its way to Super Bowl Sunday.

The development of advertising inside an agency follows a predictable pattern: project initiation, planning, copy development and review and legal clearance. The creative process (i.e., copywriting and art direction) then becomes the production process. Perhaps in this arbitrary thinking that copywriting is creative and production is technical, the assumption is made that anything creative cannot be rushed but anything "technical" can. Whatever the misperception is here, both parts of the creative process take a minimum of eight weeks. A flowchart of the production process appears as Exhibit 6.1.

The client has a similarly predictable pattern to that of advertising development inside the agency, with copy going through various levels of review and legal appraisal before it is approved for production.

In most client-agency relationships, the agency is always slightly in the lead and working against timetables of its own making. Even when things are operating at top efficiency, agency and client are out of sync, with the client running to catch up with the agency and attempting to rush internal approvals so as not to "lose time" for the agency.

The agency does indeed have a master plan or organized calendar of events. In working with agencies in the client's behalf, I have examined quite a number of different internal agency programs and found a great deal of uniformity among them. Accordingly, I took the agencies' master plan and reworked it in terms of client schedules and procedures. The system, as clients have come to call it, is nothing more or less than a mirror of the agencies' development schedule,

Exhibit 6.1
Television Commercial Production Timetable

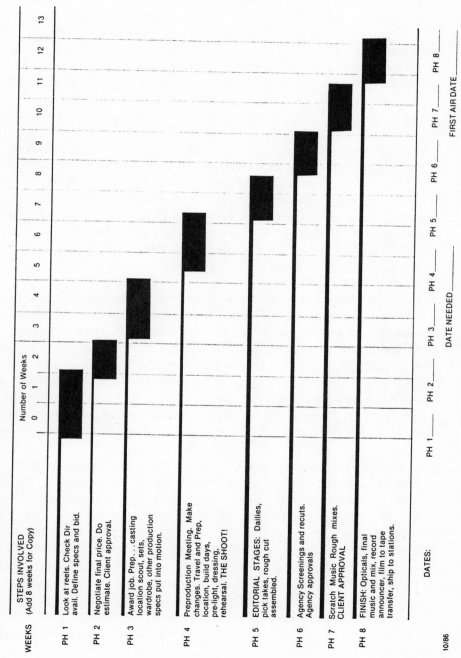

with one important difference: the system is designed to help the client stay ahead of the agency in both the copy and production process with the understood advantage that whoever leads the process controls it.

In examining internal agency systems, I noted that they had come to the consensus based on years of experience that most advertising takes eight weeks to develop as copy and another eight weeks to be produced successfully. Another two to four weeks are needed for final post-production, network clearance, duplication of materials and shipping. Twenty weeks is considered a normal time frame for the creation and production of television and print advertising, with the only exception being four weeks of production for test commercials.

I undertook a similar study of usual brand schedules. In an examination of some ninety television and print productions, the norm for client schedules was also sixteen to twenty weeks. Based on this information, I devised a planning timetable, called the commercial production project initiation form, the second step in the system (see Exhibit 6.2).

This planning timetable allows the advertiser to backtime schedules and get the agency started based on his or her own calendar of events as indicated by the quarterly calendar seen in the spending plan.

Commercial schedules are generally predicated on an air date, but such dates may not be the real first need for finished advertising. A test date, sales meeting date or management review may also be considered the necessary date of completion if this precedes the normal air date. Projects should always be initiated to coincide with the first need date for the advertising, whatever and whenever that may be.

Each major step in creative development and commercial production is outlined on the basis of usual completion schedules on the commercial production project initiation form. The appropriate number of weeks normally spent at each stage is noted. Of course, as commercials become increasingly more complex and casting demands more critical, these schedules may need to be extended. It is fair to say that not only the client but the agency itself often is falling behind in schedules with their increasingly complex review levels. As more junior creatives are pressed into service, the agency keeps kicking copy up the line to make sure it is competently designed, on strategy and the like. Copy can be written in a week, but its review inside the agency may take up to a month.

Exhibit 6.2
Commercial Production Project Initiation

DIVISION _____   DATE _____

BRAND _____   ESTIMATE NO. _____

AGENCY _____   AGENCY JOB NO. _____

RADIO_____ TV_____ TEST_____ FULLFIN._____   AGENCY ORIGINATOR _____

DESCRIPTION

_____

_____

_____

_____

WEEKS TO AIR DATE		ORIGINAL DATE	REVISED DATE
20	PROJECT INITIATION _____	_____	_____
16	FIRST COPY PRESENTATION (4)* _____	_____	_____
14	SECOND COPY PRESENTATION (2)* _____	_____	_____
12	THIRD COPY PRESENTATION (2)* _____	_____	_____
10	STORYBOARD/COPY APPD. LEGAL/NETWORK APPL. ESTIMATE APPROVED (2)* _____	_____	_____
8	PRE-PROD/CAST COMP. (2)* _____	_____	_____
7	PRODUCTION COMP. (1)* _____	_____	_____
6	FIRST SCREENING _____	_____	_____
5	SECOND SCREENING _____	_____	_____
4	TAPE APPROVED _____	_____	_____
3	NETWORK APPROVAL _____	_____	_____
2	SHIP _____	_____	_____
0	AIR DATE _____	_____	_____

*(Minimum number of weeks)

REMARKS

Using the commercial production project initiation form, the brand group and the agency can monitor their own and the other's progress and revise schedules accordingly. This is most often accomplished by the account group and forwarded to the brand manager for review. The additional benefit of this form is that it allows the brand to shift due dates early if that is needed. Granted some dates are inflexible but not as many as might be presumed. Many supposedly fixed dates can be changed, particularly when that change can be requested months in advance. Few dates are ever so carved in stone, that they cannot be shifted by a week or so. A seemingly small shift in time can save major advertisers major sums of money. An advertiser that routinely spends $10 million on production each year and routinely works on crash schedules can realistically be expected to save between $3 million and $4 million each year with a return to normal time frames.

The spending plan was designed to help organize a calendar of events by quarter. Project initiation forms are thus meant to grow out of the spending plan and its indicated advertising events. Project initiation forms for every major advertising effort should be developed in conjunction with the spending plan and reviewed by division and corporate management at the same time. This will permit them an early look at overall division schedules and help them to organize management reviews and the like at the earliest opportunity.

Although the commercial production project initiation form looks exceedingly simple and is, do not underestimate its value to you and your brand. Clients have told me that this is perhaps the most invaluable advertising control form they have ever been offered.

7

Copy and Cost Success

For clients, the copy appraisal and approval process is perhaps the most significant step in achieving great advertising for a brand at efficient costs. What are the ground rules to be observed here to ensure that you and the agency move forward in the most productive manner?

It is essential that the most professional client representative examines copy. Each division should have an advertising manager within the division or in a staff support group who has come from an agency and is knowledgeable in assessing copy and working with the agency to improve and strengthen submitted concepts. The agency will always put its best staff onto accounts whose copy and production representatives could write and produce the advertising themselves.

Copy development and assessment should be the province of this professional, with work submitted for brand and division consideration only after the advertising manager agrees that whatever the division sees can be produced for the cost indicated in the spending plan and reflects the agency's greatest skill level.

Copy meetings should be undertaken in the most disciplined manner possible. This means that decision makers should be on hand and available for comment. Meeting size should be reduced as much as possible. If brand assistants are invited to facilitate their training, they should be seen and not heard. The agency has a right to expect its work to be assessed by experienced and astute client representatives. The agency has a fatigue level. Its staff cannot be expected to listen to dozens of comments, which may or may not be worth hearing, and come away with a single reasoned idea as to what to do next.

Copy meetings should never take place unless the key decision maker is available to join the agency at some point. If this major player is not present, the agency will meet with him or her separately and eventually go only to this person, thus leapfrogging the system and effectively dismantling any semblance of division hierarchy.

Every copy meeting should begin with a reading of the copy strategy and all copy should be assessed on how rigorously it adheres to this strategy. Copy is either on strategy or it is not. If it is not, the agency should not have brought it for inspection. If the strategy is in need of change due to some new development in the marketplace, that is an entirely separate issue and should be addressed in a separate meeting or meetings.

The advertising should be consistent with ongoing campaigns. Great advertising is hard to come by, and a memorable campaign should last for years. Don't walk away from success.

All great advertising ideas can be encapsulated in a single sentence. If you do not believe your agency has one, ask the agency to present it with the print campaign. Print necessitates a headline idea and a key visual. If the advertising cannot be translated into print, a serious communications problem exists.

What are the common elements in all successful advertising? There are no absolute givens, but there are elements common to all advertising that register with memorability and persuasion. Here is what most clients find has worked for them and generated advertising that is worth producing:

1. *The product Is the hero of the advertising.* The product is featured prominently, in a favorable light and displaying strong beneficial attributes.

2. *The story line is simple.* The commercial content is structured with a beginning, middle and end. Most successful advertising is easy to follow.

3. *The product benefit is visualized.* How the product works is clearly demonstrated, often in superior comparison with other similar brands in the product category.

4. *A reason for product superiority is indicated or implied.* Some explanation for better product performance is provided to the viewers, giving them a logical or emotional "reason to believe."

5. *The advertising reflects consistency.* It appears that the simple reiteration of a single message builds awareness and confidence in the viewing audience. This is often described as being what the brand stands for.

6. *The product is introduced early and shown often.* Most successful advertising introduces the product within the first ten seconds of a thirty-second commercial. The product is seen often (at least three times) within the body of the commercial and most frequently in close-up.

7. *The product is shown in use.* The product is seen and used in a real and familiar setting. Reaction to the product is indicative of what the viewers may expect to realize themselves.

8. *The target audience is seen.* The intended customer is seen interacting with the product in a setting reflecting his or her age, character and economic background.

9. *The advertising ends with a strong product visual.* The essence of the commercial, the heart of the sale, is encapsulated in a strong closing visual statement. This is accompanied by a short declarative sentence or phrase reiterating the main promise or product claim. A short substantive "super title" is often employed duplicating what is being said.

These hallmarks of successful advertising have remained remarkably consistent through the years. How can you manage your copy meetings with the agency to make sure these elements successfully emerge in your advertising? Here are some of the ground rules to be observed to move you and the agency forward in the most productive manner possible:

1. Be open and receptive.
2. Be honest in your appraisal. Be specific.
3. Eliminate unnecessary levels of review.
4. Be consistent in what you are looking for.
5. Keep the agency aware of timetables and costs.
6. Give the agency time to respond.

Let's consider how these steps are best activated.

1. *Be open and receptive.* You hired the agency because of its track record and professionalism. Anticipate it and respect it. Good manners and objectivity are the hallmarks of any good client. Be prepared to

be surprised. Good advertising often comes at the viewer (and the client) from an unexpected angle. What may seem offbeat and a little crazy may well be the familiar simply wearing a different hat. Creativity is the name of the game here, harnessed in the service of making advertising memorable and intrusive.

2. *Be honest in your appraisal. Be specific.* The agency wants to know right away how you feel about the advertising. Some clients beat around the bush, afraid of hurting the agency's feelings. The agency should not be given the idea you like the advertising and have "just a few nits" you are concerned about when what you really mean is that the advertising is so far off the mark you would never consider making it. They should not have to return to the agency and wait for several days to have word reach them that they struck out.

Be specific as to why the advertising is not being considered further. The agency cannot work in the dark. Hopefully, it is something more than just a gut reaction on your part, but if that is what it is, say so. Intuition does play a part in this business. Perhaps you can articulate more precisely what it is about the boards submitted that seems off-base. Be as direct as you can and as specific and objective as possible.

3. *Eliminate unnecessary levels of review.* Entirely too much time is chewed up in meetings on both the agency and client side of the fence. This is one reason that both sides fall behind in the process of review and production. Organize your calendars so that the decision maker is available when needed. Do not subject the agency to day-long meetings where every brand assistant and assistant assistant gets to comment on the advertising. Committees only agree on mediocrity. Copy meetings are one reason clients have a number of offices. Shift the agency to another room, or move yourself to another area and caucus on the work under review. Everyone will feel free to be more open and candid in their remarks among their own. Brand assistants can say whatever enters their mind, and you will have saved them, your company and the agency considerable embarrassment.

4. *Be consistent in what you are looking for.* Every company has or should have a value system in place—what it believes represents good advertising (By now, I believe I have suggested some of these.) Be consistent in the way you approach the copy process and in what you choose. Do not change advertising campaigns unless the marketing and copy strategies demand such change.

Remember that brand image grows out of past advertising as much as future advertising. Your advertising heritage has been hard earned and dearly bought. There is a reason that so many advertisers are returning to older advertising slogans and campaigns. The public still remembers them and associates them with something meaningful. Sometimes the audience recognizes good advertising and remembers it better than its creators do.

Do not confuse current production techniques with inherent product drama. Any production technique may be borrowed and bought by any advertiser. If your product difference is based on a look, remember that the next advertiser in line with enough money can duplicate your advertising and go it one better. When your advertising is image driven, the agency owns it. When your advertising is product driven, you own it because the product is yours.

5. *Keep the agency aware of timetables and costs.* You have a project initiation form associated with every piece of advertising. Keep it on hand at every meeting. With every storyboard submitted for consideration, first ask the agency, "Can this be successfully accomplished within our given time frames on a normal production timetable?" Next, ask, "Can this be produced for the dollars we agreed to in our spending plan?" If they seem vague on that amount, remind them. Every storyboard presented for consideration should be accompanied by a probable cost to produce and a probable cost to air in writing. This figure must originate with the agency producer or agency cost estimator and bear their signature as having originated that number. Remember that the agency producer will soon have the responsibility for getting this advertising produced within stated cost guidelines, so involving him or her now rather than later makes good sense. Based on the number of principals so crudely drawn in on the storyboard also gives some inkling as to the cost when this advertising airs. Let the agency begin to examine the body count right now at the storyboard stage to get a quick whiff of reality. Not only do all the principals who appear in advertising get paid residuals, so do the musicians who will play the original music the agency is so casually mentioning. Based on your current media schedule, the agency can give a quick reading on how much the talent and residuals will cost. Ask for it every time a new piece of copy is presented.

Above all, insist the agency bring a clear, detailed storyboard that indicates the action and setting for the commercial. Agencies are quite casual about drawing ideas sketchily. A cable car pops up in the background or something that turns out to be the Eiffel Tower. Suddenly you are locked in to shooting in San Francisco or Paris. "The success of the board depends on it!" is the usual agency cry.

There is a need for an advertising professional to develop and strengthen copy with the agency ahead of the brand manager or company-trained marketing-advertising manager because marketing-trained managers instinctively go to the words being presented, not the pictures. Marketing managers have a wonderful facility with words. That's why agency presentations are called copy meetings. But television is a visual medium. Something like 70 percent of what we remember about a commercial is implanted through the eye. Television is a close-up medium, and selling is showing, not saying. Thus, when copy is being presented and everyone has their noses buried in the words, the real message and the cost implications of the advertising are literally passing over everyone's heads—except for the advertising manager, who is trained to think visually.

6. *Give the agency time to respond.* Don't expect the agency to react to your comments on the spot or fix whatever is troubling you. Let them have a few days to think about your comments. Make sure you have parsed out your remarks as cleanly and sharply as possible and that you have followed up your meeting with a reiteration of your thoughts in writing along with suggested areas you would like to see re-examined. Above all, don't try to suggest any changes yourself, or the agency will feel compelled to use your idea. Remember that you hired the agency for its expertise, and allow it to lead you in your thinking until you sense the agency is wandering in the wrong direction.

Most important, every copy concept has its own built-in price tag. You have been furnished with a general price indicator of costs by the 4A's display. Don't be persuaded you can buy anything and the agency will "find some way to make it happen." Every concept has its own dollar floor you cannot go below without endangering the advertising or its successful production. Get professional advice in copy and production appraisal, and use it.

8

Cutting the Costs of Test Commercials

What is the purpose of test commercials, and how is this testing best accomplished? There is a great deal of confusion in this area based on a number of variables and factors that advertisers are trying to identify before large outlays of dollars are put into commercial production.

To some degree, clients and their agencies are in an apples and oranges situation here. Commercials that have a genuine selling idea—idea-driven advertising—best lend themselves to testing. Image-driven advertising—advertising in which the execution takes the place of any selling idea—is difficult, if not impossible, to test. The rules that apply to package goods advertising, for instance, may not apply to a perfume account where the sale is mostly suggestive and ephemeral.

The difficulty arises when client and agency do not come to terms with the original purpose of their advertising and what it is intended to do. As the position of agency art director has become increasingly prominent, there has been an overall drift on the part of many agencies to position most advertising as image driven. Although, I doubt the agency would ever be so forthcoming as to say, "We don't have a competitive claim here; we're trying to establish a suggestion of worth by the size and lavishness of the execution," this may well be the primary logic at work behind the suggested advertising. And this, of course, is the catch–22 for advertisers: If there is no selling idea and executional technique is used to imply quality, the only way to validate the agency's thinking is to produce the commercials in finished form.

Should finished advertising of this nature then be tested? I don't think so. The client has willingly agreed to play along and been persuaded to give the agency its lead. The only test now applicable is sales results. The public either buys in on the act, or it doesn't (again, the valid need for fixing agency compensation based on result).

Quite a smaller number of goods and services need to be image driven, however, than current agency thinking might suggest. Even perfume advertising can be strategically positioned; that is, it can be claimed that a particular perfume lasts longer, is better liked by more people, complements individual chemistry and so forth. Positioning and uncovering a selling niche is perhaps more difficult than ever in today's competitive environment, but it can be done. Obviously it is easier for an agency to maintain that no competitive edge can be found and slide the advertising into the image camp. Image advertising requires less hard work and provides the agency and its creatives with a glossy addition to their sample, or show, reel. Agencies and creatives are seldom rewarded or noticed for solid campaigns whose only purpose is to move product (for that matter, neither are brand managers!)

If, then, there is a selling idea involved in the advertising under consideration, how can this advertising best be tested? Again, what is the purpose of test? Is it to test the idea of the advertising—its potential to persuade and generate sales—or to answer the subtler questions covered under the various subgroups: "audience reward," "commercial likability" and so forth. Whatever nourishment the advertiser finds in these indexes has little to do with the selling message or the viewer's changed perceptions and willingness to buy. Commercial likability seems to me a genuine oxymoron. Most successful commercials seem to generate an unfavorable rating with viewers by nature of their intrusiveness and memorability. No one tunes in the "Cosby Show," for instance, to catch the latest adventures of the Tidy Bowl Man. But if that advertising sticks in viewers' mind, it may well influence their buying decisions after the commercial itself is forgotten. One creative chief at a New York agency put it succinctly: "If I'm selling a man's shaving lotion, I guess the ultimate 'viewer reward' might be showing him a *Playboy* centerfold. What I don't know is if he'll bother to look at the shaving lotion in her hand while he's examining the rest of her." It is a point well taken.

By the same token, most creatives know that if they shoot off a cannon at the beginning of any spot, the viewer and viewer recall will jump, at least for the opening of the spot. But where do we go from here? Unrelated recall, or number scanning by clients without a careful study of the internals, is what many agencies fear to be the result of a client's total reliance on numbers.

For the most part, clients are a good deal more sophisticated than that. Although they may occasionally get lost in the thicket of rewards and likability they also need some assurance they are betting on the right horse. What reliance can the advertiser place on testing, and what format of testing best serves this purpose?

If the purpose of testing is to validate the strength of a selling idea or to help select among several candidates the execution that most interests and persuades the target audience, the agency must submit its advertising to test—a test produced in the simplest, most economic manner possible. The strength of the selling idea and the test situation here may be likened to a backer's audition for a Broadway show or a plot outline or treatment to sell a motion picture. As such, the most used test vehicles are animatic production, photomatics, rip-o-matics and "quick and rough/limited production."

Animatics basically are drawn art with limited movement supplied optically and a soundtrack with actors' voices, sound effects and music (hopefully stock music). Animatics can usually be accomplished for about $8,000 to $15,000 gross, depending on the number of frames drawn and the fluidity and complexity of the action being created. Almost without exception, advertisers should be urged to make use of animatics. They are the cheapest, clearest, most serviceable unit of test. Some agencies insist animatics do not work. Their concerns are generally centered on the static image, the use of art instead of photographs and the lack of production values. Other agency creatives agree that animatics can be used in a limited number of situations, excluding special categories such as beauty, food and celebrities. Let's investigate these objections.

Consider the static image. Animatics do not have the absolute freedom of the full-finished commercial, but does this mean that the advertising message cannot be relayed to the viewer? If it did, no advertiser would ever use print, which does not move at all. The argument that certain categories such as beautiful hair, for instance, cannot be achieved with artwork is equally suspect. For years, Breck carried its full print campaign using an artist's rendition of beautiful hair.

What about the lack of production value, nuances, the look of the advertising being the mechanism that drives the sale? This argument is fallacious. As any knowledgeable creative director knows, production value has nothing to do with the communication efficacy of the sale. There is no correlation between the lavishness of production (or its lack) and the idea of the advertising. No amount of good or even great production value can salvage a bad idea. Conversely, it takes almost a willful amount of bad production to obscure a great selling idea. Hollywood has known this for years. Stars and elaborate production values may bring the audience in for the first week or so, but ultimately the success of the picture depends on audience word of mouth. It is the content of the material that ensures its success. Production values may give surface gloss, but nobody comes out of a Broadway show humming the sets.

What about celebrity talent? Recently one of my clients was interested in securing the services of a well-known model-personality for a food product. The question was, "Will women find her believable as a spokeperson and her winning figure attributable to eating our product?" The agency rationale went something like this: An animatic won't work; we have to see her figure. A photomatic is better, but it still doesn't allow us to catch her in movement, get the sparkle of her personality and the appetite appeal of the food itself. Accordingly the agency bid out the job as a limited production and a photomatic. The proposed cost of the limited production was $80,000. The cost of the proposed photomatic was $55,000. The agency posed these as rock-bottom prices and was still concerned over the loss of "production values" to enhance the looks and performance of their celebrity presenter—all logical and persuasive arguments except that the original point of the test had been simply one of believability: Do women buy this celebrity as a spokesperson? That question could be simply answered, and it was by using an existing still of the celebrity in a bathing suit and creating a rough print ad with the model talking about the product. The print concept was used in a mall intercept and successfully answered the advertiser's concerns—at a cost of $5,600. Even better, in addition to saving money on the test, the agency was well on its way to developing a print ad for the campaign.

Rip-o-matics are scrap art or materials previously shot for other advertising. Clearly the advertiser is at risk if such advertising runs anywhere on air and talent is not paid. Another danger exists in that rip-o-matics already indicate a level of production that immediately becomes associated with the advertising. The director who is being sold along with the rip-o-matic may not be affordable. Agencies often sell an idea and a technique or director as a package. This represents a risk to the uninformed client.

Photomatics and *quick and rough/limited production* both represent scaled down "live" shootings. Photomatics are accomplished using a 35mm "still" camera with the resulting photographs manipulated optically much in the manner of animatics to give a semblance of movement. Tape or 16mm are the preferred sources in quick and rough. Shootings are arbitrarily limited in time, scope and production finish to capture the basic communication idea as inexpensively as possible.

Whenever actual production is attempted, however, the temptation is great to make the effort as finished as possible. The result may well be runaway costs, obviating original intent.

Unless the selling idea is so weak it is totally dependent on production values to mask its flaws, or so ephemeral it can only be suggested by lavish production to suggest worth, animatics represent the cheapest, quickest way to test the validity of a selling idea. Verify this contention for yourself with whatever testing facility you currently use. Let their experience be your guide.

It has been my experience (and the experience of a number of major advertisers) that animatic testing, the cheapest form of testing format available, will serve you well across most category lines. Several years ago, a major advertiser decided to determine the efficacy of animatics versus photomatics and limited production. Accordingly he tested in each format and then compared test scores to the numbers generated by testing the full-finished advertising itself. Fifty commercials were analyzed, test to full-finished counterpart. The results? Regardless of the testing format, all of the test commercials scored within five percent of the full-finished advertising. Given the norms of testing, that 5 percent variance would occur if the same full-finished advertising was tested twice. In short, there was no variance anywhere down the line.

Ultimately, the major source of friction between agency and advertiser is not the subjecting of advertising to test but the way in which test results are handled. No agency likes a report card mentality at work inside client headquarters. But if testing is done as a learning experience to separate the wheat from the chaff, it is useful. Perhaps you, the client, should suggest that the agency itself be in charge of testing.

If testing is a learning experience—to be a tool in furthering judgment, not a replacement for it—who is better than the agency to discover where copy deficiencies lie? Given the opportunity to generate its own diagnostics, fiddle with the advertising, fix it and expand it, the agency may then be in a better position to take the client through the learning experience and arrive in hand with certifiably proved results indicating probable success.

Certainly with the average commercial costing the equivalent of a house in the suburbs, the client is entitled to a close inspection of the property before signing on the dotted line.

9

Cutting Costs at the Storyboard Stage

Until now your appraisal of the storyboard has been an examination of the impact of the communications—and rightly so. Now examine the advertising in terms of its internal demands that drive production and fuel higher costs. Remember that there is no correlation between advertising expense and advertising effectiveness. Production costs are driven only by internal demands, which may or may not play any part in the successful execution of the advertising.

What should you be looking for to cut costs before production gets underway? Here are some classic cost-cutting opportunities.

Question the need for multiple scenes. Count the number of scene changes reflected in your storyboard. Every time action jumps to a new set or location, that set or location must be built, found, reached, lighted, propped, equipment and people moved and the scene staged and shot. Each new setup will take from four to six hours to accomplish. As a rough rule of thumb, put an eventual cost of $75,000 against each scene shown on the storyboard.

What is the value of multiple scenes? Scene changes divert viewer attention and interrupt the flow of the story and the logic of the sale. Unless you want to register the idea that "everyone is doing it," try to restructure action to take place in a single uniform setting.

Question the need for location shootings. It may be cheaper to go to a location than to try to replicate a large set piece on stage. But is going on location for variety a worthwhile expense? Each location day will eventually cost about $95,000, plus another $12,000 in agency travel and per diem. If you are selling a car, for instance, does it matter if the camera lovingly inspects it in close-up or sees it driving on a nearby street or parked in front of the Eiffel Tower? What are you selling? What is your focus?

What about the dollar economies of overseas locations? Shooting overseas is inherently more expensive. The average cost of a shooting day is just about double the cost of shooting inside the country once travel costs have been factored in. Economies due to dollar exchange rates depend on the soundness of the dollar at that particular moment. "Runaway production" does not automatically generate real savings. Moreover, cheaper talent buyouts in overseas markets are fast disappearing, and casting is a good deal more time-consuming and costly. "American types" may be hard to come by (even in Canada), especially if they have to speak.

Question the need for night scenes. Unless they are dramatically necessary, night scenes are always more difficult to light and shoot and often require overtime hours. If possible, move the action to an interior and suggest night by letting light fall off outside windows.

Question the need for large interiors. Don't build them, and don't rent them unless the action demands their use. Avoid shooting in large public places—train stations, airline terminals, skating rinks and so forth. The entire area will have to be lighted and filled with actors and extras, special permits will always be required and some means of crowd control must be in place—plus travel time to and from these places is at your expense, and steals time away from the shooting schedule.

Question the need for all exterior scenes. Shooting outdoors exposes talent, product and packages to sun, wind, rain, traffic and the general public. All can play havoc with schedules. Skin, hair and food advertising attempted outdoors puts clients at risk. Always have the agency producer work out realistic terms and agreement as to "weather days" should you be rained or blown out on a shoot day. If possible, shoot indoors with a suggestion of an exterior location achieved through propping, lighting, backdrops or large windows.

Question the need for multiple actors. Costs operate exponentially in production. The more actors are needed, the more time will be spent in casting, costuming, makeup, lighting and directing these people and the bigger the sets will have to be to hold them. Additionally, the more principals are involved in a commercial, the more money it will cost to air the advertising each time it is shown.

Everyone who is identifiable, uses or reacts to the product is a principal. Performers hired as extras who are recognized will be upgraded to the level of principal. Principals earn the highest residual rates as dictated by union scale. Every time the commercial plays on network—each network—the player gets another payment. If he or she appears in the same evening on all three networks, three payments are generated. Reuse charges for the advertising will eventually be as costly as the original production. Rewrite the advertising if necessary to lower the number of actors required.

Question the need for original music. The use of original music will cost approximately $20,000 in composition, recording and talent fees. All musicians and singers are paid residuals each time the commercial plays. If your copy is "wall-to-wall words," chances are you don't need music at all. Before you are persuaded to commission original music, examine stock music, which can be purchased for about $1,000 and has no composition, arrangement fees, permission rights or talent and residual costs associated with its use.

What about buying rights to familiar music? Unless the music is in the public domain, buying rights to it is almost prohibitively expensive, there is little or no room for negotiation here. Moreover, buying the rights to the song does not buy the performer usually associated with it. No previously recorded versions may be used unless all musicians and singers contracted for that recording have been identified and paid once again. They too must be paid ongoing residual fees.

Question the need for special effects and animation. Special visual devices always represent a step back from reality. Unless there is a need to demonstrate how a product works that cannot be achieved by shooting the real object in action with extreme close-up and slow motion, or you are developing a continuing character, such as the Jolly Green Giant or Dow's Scrubbing Bubbles, remember that special effects and animation may well be borrowed interest. They are always time-consuming (six to twelve weeks), and require the services of a limited pool of highly specialized technicians and equipment. Atop whatever is being spent for live action, special visuals can cost anywhere from $60,000 to $400,000. Integrating live action and animation is a tedious, costly and time-consuming business. Rushing schedules in this area can be disastrously expensive.

Question the need for children and animals. Both are natural attention getters, which may or may not work in your behalf. Special personnel are always required, and shooting schedules will expand to however long it takes to catch the action. Having children and animals included in the action only for visual interest is a bad idea.

Question the need for shooting additional versions. Usually this is generated when some legal question arises. Postpone shooting until you have resolved the legal question. No storyboard should move into the production stage until the board has received internal, agency and network legal clearance. If one network finds your advertising unacceptable, perhaps proper wordsmithing can satisfy it, and then make that the single commercial you shoot.

Shooting additional versions for any reason is time-consuming and costly. The only exception to this rule that represents a client savings is in shooting new and non-new versions of a commercial. A product may be referred to as new for only six months after product introduction. Dialogue and product shots should both be done in new and non-new versions. There is no additional talent charge for these alternate versions on the shooting day or in residual fees in airing.

Talent payments may be reduced in airing shorter versions of the same advertising if this is accomplished as a mechanical lift in editing rather than shooting a separate adapt. This is something that many agency account groups and even producers are not familiar with. One client alerted to this fact asked his agency not to proceed with reshooting a scene as an adapt but to accomplish the shorter version as a mechanical lift. Eliminating a one-word change for the adapt saved $12,000 in shooting and editing and an additional $75,000 in residual fees.

As an overview in final storyboard examination, try to put yourself in the viewers' shoes. Remember that they are merely looking for information to help them make a better buying decision. They are not a captive audience or a particularly attentive one. Simplicity and straightforward communication of a single idea is all a fifteen-second or thirty-second commercial can hope to carry successfully.

Television is a close-up medium. Your product should be the star of your commercial. Everything that does not focus attention on the product should be suspect. Try to look at the storyboard with the simplicity of what the camera demands to see. The camera is the viewers' eyes. Selectivity is the key to memorability.

What else should you do in your final assessment of advertising before giving the agency the go-ahead in production?

Time the advertising. Put a stopwatch against the entire commercial.

Read it aloud. Nearly every successful commercial has air in it; reading time runs two to three seconds short in a thirty-second spot. These few seconds allow the director and actors to include bits of business, react naturally and allow the commercial to retain some warmth.

Since you began the copy process, you may have added words for legal reasons that have exhausted time limits or necessitate a reading as rapid as machine-gun fire. See if the copy can be simplified and shortened.

Time your product shots. Is there sufficient dialogue or announcer copy to permit the camera to hold on your product naturally? Is there justification in the action for the product to be naturally introduced and seen in tight close-up? Two actors and your product in a medium shot is not a product close-up.

The best judge of all this is the agency producer, who is able to provide pertinent cost information on every element in the advertising? Never proceed into production without his or her assessment and assurance that the storyboard will successfully translate onto film with clarity and charm and in line with your budget. It is the producer's responsibility to bring you safely through the production process and out the other side with your selling idea and budget intact. Don't leave home without them.

10

The Roles of the Writer, Art Director and Producer

To maintain any sort of realistic cost control in the production of advertising—television, radio or print—you, the client, need to have a frank discussion about the importance you place on costs and the role of the producer in controlling them.

The rise of the art director since the 1960s and the blurring of the responsibilities of the art director and producer over the past twenty years has played a significant part in advertising impact, advertising credibility and advertising costs. The extent to which the art director has been allowed to work autonomously within the agency and free of client control is the extent to which shootings have become increasingly costly and inefficient.

In the 1968 4A's Broadcast Committee Report on Television Cost Controls, the agencies themselves noted:

> The art director in recent years has become more and more involved in production . . . to the extent that he has, this has tended to increase costs. . . . Today's increased costs are the inevitable result of a highly competitive striving for creative excellence in an area where the specialized talent supply is very limited and personal points of view often dominate business decisions. The intensity of competition among agencies for creative pre-eminence . . . [changes] the costs of commercials over and above the normal cost of living increases.

In 1985, an ANA report on production costs and factors that drive up production expense again squarely placed the blame on agency creatives—writer–art director teams who call the shots without the active involvement of the agency producer to provide necessary balance and stability in the process of commercial production: "The influence agency producers have on costs is limited. They lack authority over creatives, and because of that, the number of highly qualified agency line producers has declined. . . . Creatives have little motivation to save dollars. . . . There are too many [creative] layers, too many revisions."

Also noted in the ANA report as to why production costs were rising was the inexperience and culpability of clients: "Inexperienced product managers find it difficult to resist senior agency people. . . . Poor planning leads to rushed production. . . . Advertisers set no limits on costs going in, then complain loudly when the final bill arrives."

In a nutshell, the ANA report summarized what has been going wrong since the 1960s: The advertiser has let inexperienced brand managers pick the advertising and authorize their attendant costs. The agency creatives, operating unchecked and unmanaged, have demanded absolute control over who is picked to shoot the advertising and how it should be accomplished. These decisions have been made with little or no regard for the cost. When any questions on the efficiency or inefficiency of the shooting are raised, the subject is handed to the producer and the production department, who have had little or no authority over creative decision making.

What is the advertiser to do? First, it is important to put decision-making power into the hands of experienced advertising experts working in the company. Second, it is important to provide the agency with strict cost guidelines. Third, it is important to clarify that the appropriate staff assume appropriate tasks to ensure that the planning, execution and costs of the production are handled as realistically and efficiently as possible. This begins with an understanding of the roles of the writer, art director and producer.

The writer creates the scene, characters, situation and dialogue and a rough outline of how the action should be captured by the camera. The art director contributes to the visual artistry of the scenes, the overall design, graphic elements and visual texture. The producer takes these ideas and puts a physical and cost dimension to the project. Everyone is responsible for creating advertising that is successfully produced within the budget set by the advertiser. The account group acting in the client's behalf is responsible for taking the ideas generated by the creative team and discussing them with the producer and agency business manager to see if the advertising is within target range of the client's budget. If the concept is too expensive, the producer must simplify the concept or reject it. The account group then sees that the advertising is restructured or scrapped and another execution written to bring creative requirements in line with the budget. Clearly the sophistication and professionalism of the creative group should be measured by its ability to create advertising that can be successfully and handsomely produced given the dollar restraints imposed by the client. If the creatives cannot do this, they should be recognized as unsophisticated and unprofessional and taken off the business at the client's request.

There is another reason to want these people off your business as quickly as possible: There is every likelihood that creatives who cannot focus on advertising costs also cannot focus on advertising content. In my experience, these creative teams are the ones who routinely present the client with the costliest image advertising having little to do with product benefit, performance, differentiation or selling effectiveness. The extent to which the creative team insists on putting its character imprint on the advertising is the extent to which the product's character and individuality is submerged. The agency owns the advertising; the advertiser is held hostage creatively and financially.

At the start of the year, it is important for the client at the highest possible level to speak to agency management at its highest levels about costs, waste and production efficiency. You, the client, must demand that the most senior producer at the agency control director selection, all elements associated with the production, the editing and the costs associated with production. If the agency demurs or mentions a "team concept" (a code phrase meaning that the creatives assume production authority), then it should be established that all production responsibility rests with the creative group, including responsibility for the quality and costs associated with production. Since the agency has chosen not to enlist the expertise of its own producers, it should be expected to absorb all cost overruns.

I can already hear howls of protest and cries of woe arising from many agencies. "We can't work under these conditions!" "We're being put into a creative straitjacket!" "No creatives will want to work on your business if they're subject to these restrictions!" Well, what restrictions are we talking about? The agency insists that the client is responsible for costs by setting a dollar limit on the advertising. The agency then insists it must have total responsibility for spending that money. Nowhere in this agreement is it written that if the agency mismanages its costs, the client is responsible to give the agency more money to cover the dollar shortfall caused by that mismanagement. Worse, since the agency is getting a commission (17.65 percent) on everything it spends, the agency is actually making more money by wasting money than by being disciplined in its efforts.

The role of the producer is to bring reality to bear on what was only concept before. The producer must be responsible for picking those people in front of and behind the camera who are most suited to the demands of the advertising, artistically and economically. The producer must have the responsibility for making sure the board translates from paper to film, that the selling idea is skillfully visualized and that it is completely realized in terms of content, look and value.

You may be wondering if this insistence on the producer's running the production is not overstated or stumbling over rather arbitrary definitions of who does what. Ask your own advertising consultant his or her opinion, or ask the director at your current or next shooting. What you will hear are more examples than you care to know of self-indulgent creative teams' turning the simplest shooting into a parody of creative excess: creative teams' spending days looking at directors' reels and ultimately picking the wrong director; creative teams' insisting on using the hottest current director, suitable or not, and then refusing to listen to this person; endless wrangling on the set over questions of lighting or costuming or the red car versus the black car in a scene in which the car is a minimal prop; lighting requirements so demanding that each setup takes ten hours to light and the shot itself runs two seconds in the finished commercial.

Where is production expertise in all this? On one set I visited, shooting was yet to begin at 2 P.M., although the job was supposed to start at 8 A.M. The art director and writer and director were still discussing whether the actress should be wearing a blue or a white robe. Because the job was considered so important by the client, the producer assigned was the vice president in charge of production for the agency; she was not on the set. The art director had asked her to make herself useful and see if she could find some batteries for his cellular phone.

These examples are not the exception to the rule; they are the rule when many creative teams are given jurisdiction over the production planning, shooting and editing of advertising. While creative egos are flexed, the production meter keeps running. All of those people standing around the set are being paid by the hour whether the camera turns or not. Much overtime expense—perhaps $30,000 a day—has been built into the budget in advance to ensure that the creatives will not be rushed into making a decision on the set. What is not mentioned is that the professional producer makes those decisions prior to the shooting day so the additional $30,000 is not needed.

This is the arrogant display, the waste and inefficiency and creative coddling that have driven costs up 250 percent since 1980. This waste is what a well-organized producer must be empowered to stop.

11

Moving into the Production Process

Let's review briefly what has already been accomplished in your efforts to achieve successful advertising at effective levels of spending.

You have analyzed your past performance and that of the agency. You have worked to resolve any operating problems and clarified responsibility within your division and inside the agency. You have discovered and articulated a value equation—that point at which copy has proved most successful and costs most moderate. You have developed a realistic spending plan, setting spending levels for every major category of expense. You have established a quarterly calendar of events and are controlling time by your use of the project initiation form. You have determined the probable success of your advertising through testing, and you have managed test costs to produce that advertising as inexpensively as possible. You have developed an ongoing value equation with your examination of test results and your examination of a probable cost to produce and a probable cost to air. You have insisted the agency manage its affairs intelligently and that proper roles in the creative-production process be observed. All of these elements of the system are really the underpinning of an effective copy management program.

You are now at the stage of approving final copy and beginning the planning stages of production. This is where the system shifts to one of production management. The tools at your disposal now are the pre-production agenda, the specifications sheet, the AICP form and overscale contracts.

How actively you participate in the production area should be determined by your experience. The less knowledgeable you are, the better you will be served by maintaining distance. The agency has been given the responsibility for the successful creation of advertising and the proper administration of costs. The more you, the client, decide to participate, the more your involvement reduces total agency accountability. And the more deeply you involve yourself in the minutiae of production, the less likely you are to retain your overall view and perspective of the advertising and what it is meant to accomplish in your marketing efforts. Participation gives away authority. For that reason, marketing managers at all levels should reserve the right of final decision making for themselves and send a production agent ahead in their service.

This individual may be the advertising manager already in place, a member of the staff support group hired for his or her production experience or a consultant hired on a retainer basis to oversee all elements of the advertising and production process for your company.

There are perhaps a dozen consultants working at the national level who have established a verifiable track record with clients and agencies. Some are called advertising consultants, some production consultants and others cost consultants. The difference in these titles refers to differences in their grasp of the advertising process and the sphere of activity in which they most comfortably fit.

Advertising consultants work most comfortably through the entire process, and their level of experience permits them to work effectively with all levels of client and agency management. Their contributions will generate the greatest savings possible on an ongoing basis with the least amount of friction internally and between client and agency.

Production consultants' activities are mostly bound by the production process itself. They will have little input into analyzing and restructuring creative efforts and will not be granted access to key decision makers inside the agency. Savings generated by development of overriding policies and procedures pertaining to production may be accomplished. They will be welcome at actual production events: bidding, pre-production and shootings.

Cost consultants are perhaps the least effective participants. Their background and capabilities preclude association with senior corporate and agency management, and their sphere of influence is only in the area of examining costs already generated by agency and production company. Generally regarded as cost-cutting technicians, they may well enter the picture too late, creating considerable friction and displaying less than satisfactory sensitivity to creative intent. They will attempt to reduce costs by somewhat arbitrary means and usually position themselves as "keeping the agency honest."

In terms of overall savings, the advertising consultant may be expected to save the client 30 percent or more of the advertising budget, especially in the first year and particularly in establishing ongoing policies and contracts more favorable to the client. The production consultant may be expected to realize savings at about the 20 percent level. The cost consultant will show savings of about 10 percent on a per job basis.

Any consultant must not only examine initial costs but final actual costs as well. The agency can indeed backload dollars, driving up the entire production budget 20 to 30 percent in final client billings.

Assessing your own experience and current costs will help you decide whether you need professional assistance. Your agency can provide a fair and accurate appraisal of all consultants working in the marketplace and should be asked about possible candidates. Assessing your agency and its production expertise will also help in your decision as to whether a consultant is needed.

12

Setting the Pre-Production Agenda

Most so-called production problems are actually copy problems or the late realization, usually in the screening room, that differing points of view were not resolved prior to the start of production. Why does this happen, and how can it be eliminated?

The storyboard is only the roughest indication of what is to be shot. The significance of each scene, each shot, may be perceived differently by every person who looks at the board. Everyone has an idea of what the commercial should look like and is already "running the film in his head." Unfortunately, these "private screenings" cannot be viewed by anyone else.

The key to a successful production depends on the precise articulation and unanimous agreement as to what is desired in terms of physical look and emotional timbre. This must be accomplished on a scene-by-scene, sometimes shot-by-shot basis. What is the purpose of each scene? How does it contribute to the whole? What is the tonality of the advertising? This is the purpose and importance of the pre-production meeting agenda (see Exhibit 12.1).

Let's review the importance of the categories indicated on this form.

"Agency Originator" refers to the agency producer acting in concert with the creatives, the creative director and the account group. (The account group may officially send this document forward.)

"Casting Objectives" should reflect the target audience in age, look, personality, economic background, life-style and so on. If you have anyone specific in mind or can refer to someone, that is, a "Bette

Exhibit 12.1
Commercial Production/Pre-Production Meeting Agenda

AGENCY: _____ DATE: _____

PRODUCT: _____

COMMERCIAL TITLE(S): _____

AGENCY ORIGINATOR: _____

I.   CASTING-OBJECTIVES

_____
_____
_____
_____

II. WARDROBE DESCRIPTIONS

_____
_____
_____
_____

III. LOCATION DESCRIPTION

_____
_____
_____
_____

IV. PRESENTATION OF STORYBOARD

  A. COMMERCIAL TONALITY

_____
_____
_____
_____

Exhibit 12.1 (continued)

B. CHARACTER RELATIONSHIP

_____

_____

_____

C. PACING

_____

_____

_____

D. ATMOSPHERE

_____

_____

_____

V. OBJECTIVES AND SUMMARY OF EACH SCENE

SCENE I _____

_____

_____

SCENE II _____

_____

_____

SCENE III _____

_____

_____

SCENE IV _____

_____

_____

SCENE V _____

_____

_____

Midler type," you will contribute to getting casting underway faster and in a much more disciplined manner. Some clients have blind spots, and here is the time to spell them out, with no apologies, that is, "No Redheads Need Apply!" If you can supply a headsheet from a previous casting session or specifically want to see someone in casting, include the person's name.

"Wardrobe Descriptions" should be as specific as possible. A picture torn from a magazine may be helpful.

"Location Description" should be specific as to what is wanted but not necessarily where. A beautiful beach and palm trees does not necessarily mean California. Florida, Puerto Rico or even Hawaii can be cheaper, especially if business has been slow there.

"Commercial Tonality" speaks to the attitude behind the advertising and its feel: news announcement flavor, warm and folksy, slyly humorous or something else.

"Character Relationship" is intended to reveal something the board may only hint at: "Father and son love each other, but son feels Dad is hopelessly out of date and out of touch. His gibes are playfully intended."

"Pacing" refers to length of shots, cutting tempo and what may influence it—for example, "Visually, this will be a series of cuts between each scene and in tempo with the musical beat. The cumulative effect will be a smooth-flowing image."

"Atmosphere" should indicate the overall look of the advertising: fresh, lively, clean and so forth.

"Objectives and Summary of Each Scene" is designed to describe specifically the important contribution of each particular scene: "to establish the relationship of father and son" or "We establish the car as their common bond," for example. Each scene should be described fully enough so that communication takeaway by the viewer is clearly delineated.

If a previous commercial reflects everything you want in the new advertising, please indicate this: "Duplicate the look and feel of the 'Houseboat' spot done in June." If you got along famously with a director on the last shooting, instruct the agency to bid him or her again. He or she already has a track record of knowing what you want and what you want to spend. (Creative groups currently have a fashion of loving a director's work and then never using the person again. Encourage them to rethink this curious notion).

None of this information is designed to diminish director contribution later. How he or she accomplishes these aims is his or her decision. What you want accomplished is yours.

A detailed description of product shots should also accompany the pre-production meeting agenda, specifying anything that has not been previously covered, for example, "Bottle is to be seen in package and standing beside package (2 shots). Giant Size is to be used."

Everyone who will be involved in decision making on the advertising should read and revise the pre-production meeting agenda until it accurately and completely reflects client and agency thinking.

Only one copy of the agenda should be sent back to the agency. Importantly, everyone who sees and contributes to this document should sign off on it with initials. This should prove helpful later when someone from the client or agency arrives in the screening room and begins complaining: "This is nowhere close to what I had in mind." Anyone who has not made his or her wishes known until now needs to be reminded of the fact.

The pre-production meeting agenda is designed to provide specific guidance to the agency producer and to enable him or her to give detailed specifications to the production companies that will be bidding on the job.

As production moves forward, the agenda will serve as the backbone of the pre-production meeting and a call report of that meeting. The importance of this document in articulating creative intent and serving as a primary cost control device cannot be overestimated.

13

Cutting Costs at the Specifications Stage

Specifications are buying instructions to the production companies that are being asked to bid on your commercial. Production companies and their directors break out into predictable cost ranges, and these are well known to agencies and producers in advance of seeing numbers from them. Your pre-determination of cost ceilings has already precluded certain companies that always command premium prices regardless of the work to be done.

The words specifications and specificity grow from the same root and should be your key to the degree of exactitude required in the process. You have already taken a large step forward through the implementation of the pre-production agenda. What other steps should be taken now to ensure that buying instructions reflect your concentrated efforts to buy wisely and eliminate waste?

Insist that specifications be developed by a knowledgeable producer and reviewed by the appropriate business affairs managers and cost estimators available inside the agency. These are highly trained, highly skilled professionals meant to be of service to the producer and you.

If you have an in-house production unit or a consultant on retainer, make sure they have input and are in agreement with the specs before release. This pre-bid discussion may be handled by telephone.

Make sure adequate time exists to avoid rush in the bidding process and that adequate time exists to rebid, if necessary. One to two weeks is adequate.

Make sure that specifications are written and not communicated orally to all production companies. This guarantees that all suppliers are getting the same information and avoids agencies' possible rigging of the bid.

Don't forget that the agency's basic drive is to seek perfection. This is not necessarily bad, but it must be tempered by reality and a recognition of your budget.

The bidding process is a negotiating process. There are no "right" costs for anything. What you get on film should always look like more than what you actually paid.

There are some basic agreements that you and the agency should have in place prior to the start of bidding. Here are some pertinent points of view that represent the best thinking of producers, business managers and consultants working in the industry today. They may be considered tough but fair demands and a realistic client posture. These buying policies should be enforced and subject to reconsideration only after the agency has made a thorough, reasoned and convincing argument based specifically on the work in hand.

1. *Eliminate the pre-light day.* The pre-light day is a fairly recent invention of creative groups and production companies. It is necessary only when a commercial is so extraordinarily complex that rehearsal time is needed prior to shooting. Eliminating the pre-light day will usually save $20,000 to $30,000.

2. *Eliminate multiple shooting days.* Most commercials not overly complex in writing require only one day to complete. Until just a few years ago, a sixty-second and a thirty-second commercial were being shot in one day, with no overtime. Some agencies are now requesting two days and a pre-light day for a fifteen-second spot. Every day eliminated saves a minimum $100,000.

3. *Eliminate overtime built into the original bid.* A properly planned and executed commercial seldom needs more than eight hours to shoot. Building overtime into the bid before the commercial ever gets in front of the cameras artificially drives costs up as much as 100 percent. A fourteen-hour day is roughly the equivalent in cost of two normal eight-hour days when time and a half and double-time rates are in effect for union crews. Building overtime into the bid up front permits work to expand to fill the time allotted. Overtime can always be negotiated on set at the shooting if it is really needed. Cutting a fourteen-hour day to 8 hours will cut a $300,000 job to about $200,000.

4. *Eliminate overscale talent in front of and behind the camera.* There

are thousands of talented people working in the industry who will be delighted to work for scale. Union scale rates in most categories have increased 150 to 200 percent (or more) in recent years. Overscale talent multiplies those increases times three and in many cases times five.

5. *Eliminate large sets and stages.* Most sets are overbuilt in size and complexity and thus require larger stages to hold them. Few sets need all four walls or additional rooms off the major set piece. By making some changes in set requirements and staging, a client recently reduced the gross costs of a single commercial from $258,382 to $139,242. The difference was undetectable, even by the agency's admission.

6. *Eliminate overpriced equipment.* Few shootings require the elaborate rigs, cameras, lenses and lighting seen at most shootings today. Equipment packages at much lower rates will turn in superior results.

7. *Eliminate versions of commercials.* Exploring every variation of how the advertising could be done is another example of "the pursuit of the perfect :30." Eliminate versions by clarifying goals, getting legal matters ironed out in advance and "not covering it for the boss several different ways." Each additional version eliminated will save between $10,000 and $20,000.

8. *Eliminate flying talent from coast to coast.* It has become fashionable to fly New York directors and talent to the West Coast and vice versa. Eliminating this practice will save at least $10,000. Use talent at their home base or pick someone else.

9. *Eliminate star directors.* Hundreds of topnotch directors are available for every kind of shooting. Constant use of a handful clustered in New York City has developed the myopic vision that they are the only acceptable directors. The star director brings outsized expectations and costs. Eliminating a star director from contention usually reduces costs by about one-third.

10. *Negotiate the 35 percent markup.* Markup represents the profit margin production companies put atop their raw costs. Thirty-five percent was a standard figure developed years ago before the invention of the AICP form. This form generated by the production companies themselves already turns back to the advertiser costs that formerly were absorbed by production companies as *their* cost of doing business. Markups can be negotiated at rates starting at 26 percent. Push your agencies to negotiate sharply.

11. *Eliminate production company markup on insurance.* Every pro-

duction company insures itself against possible malfunction of equipment and unforeseeable difficulties at a rate equivalent to 2 or 3 percent of the job. They then put their company markup (26 to 35 percent) atop this number and pass it along to the agency, which marks it up another 17.65 percent. Insist that the production company eliminate markup on insurance. If your company is a self-insurer, investigate whether you need insurance at all.

12. *Eliminate single bids.* Many agencies maintain that only one director is right for a job. This is never the case. Some agencies maintain there is not enough time to bid multiple production companies. This is nonsense. Jobs are being bid simultaneously at all houses asked to compete. Three or six houses competitively bidding against each other will reduce costs as much as 40 percent. On the average job, this is a savings of about $50,000.

13. *Eliminate fees for storyboards.* You should not be paying the agency to develop storyboards. This is included in their costs of overhead. You should not be paying production companies for shooting boards developed in the course of planning the job.

14. *Eliminate post-production costs in planning.* Neither you nor the agency knows if elaborate post-production will be required until the film is in a rough assemblage. Pay only for editorial completion, and then handle further work as an overage. You may generate savings of about $20,000 per job by working on a pay-as-you-go basis.

15. *Eliminate color-corrected product.* Most packages and cans are camera ready and need no color correction. You can save from $4,000 by avoiding unnecessary color correction.

These are just a few of the ideas that should be pursued with the agency. When you are assembling a complete advertising manual, review, update and distribute your entire buying strategy and contractual understandings with the agency and suppliers to all divisions, managers and agency personnel.

Some other opportunities are also available in holding the line on costs. I have already suggested that you shoot in pools and ask the agency to write and produce advertising in quantity—two or three commercials at a time. This is a genuine opportunity to lower costs by 30 percent or more.

I have also suggested you reuse elements whenever possible: vignettes, demonstrations and product shots. This is not only an opportunity to reduce costs but to promote memorability. Using a short encapsulation of your product benefit over and over provides you with a signature shot that is yours alone and generates registration of your product and its reason for being.

Examine resources available outside the major production centers of New York City and Los Angeles. There are thriving and imaginative production centers in Boston, Chicago, Dallas, Miami, Orlando, Philadelphia, Phoenix, Toronto and elsewhere. Unless your board demands high-fashion or special effects, have your agency routinely bid these production facilities. Costs may be cut in half by moving out of the New York–Los Angeles axis.

Examine what you shoot on. For shooting beauty and food, 35mm film is nearly always preferred, but 16mm and tape can dramatically cut costs through the use of lighter, more portable equipment, smaller crew size and other benefits.

There are very few absolute "givens" or "must haves" in commercial production. Ask the agency to show you the handiwork of directors with whom you may not be familiar and production results achieved on 16mm and tape. Remember that it is your money and your standards the agency is attempting to satisfy.

14

Buying Options: Firm Bid and Cost Plus Fixed Fee

The advertiser is allowed two choices in buying production: firm bid and cost plus fixed fee. Each has its advocates. Each has its benefits and disadvantages.

Essentially, the firm bid approach is based on a competitive bidding situation. Three or more suppliers are given the specifications, the board is discussed at some length in terms of creative intent and options available and the suppliers bid against each other for who can do the job more economically as well as more effectively for the money. Whoever comes in lowest gets the job, and the budget is frozen at that level.

Cost plus intimates that a specific director and production company have already been selected for their creative merits and are about to enter the production process as partners. The specifications will grow out of the discussions of creative intent, with a dollar threshold indicated. The production company will buy what is needed and wanted with a clear articulation of the costs associated with every element. Atop these costs will be placed a fixed fee or production house markup for administration, overhead and profit margin—anywhere from 26 to 35 percent.

In the cost-plus situation, the production company must provide vendor receipts to the agency on everything purchased, and its books may be audited at the completion of the work. Auditing is not permitted with a firm bid contract. The critical difference here is that in the firm bid situation, the production company keeps any money not spent, but it will have to absorb any cost overruns unless the client and agency can be shown to have changed specifications and requirements for the work to be done substantially after the job was underway. Additional costs are then subject to discussion and negotiation as to who pays what.

Cost plus fixed fee offers clients a great deal more control over how their dollars are spent provided that the agency has a knowledgeable producer assigned to the job who will stay with it and that both agency and client managers are direct and clear on what they want and conversant with production terms, processes and legitimate cost ranges. Unless this is the case, the costs of production remain open-ended. In a cost-plus situation, this is analogous to the agency's being handed the client's credit card and instructed to return it only when the agency is done shopping.

In cost-plus situations where the client does not have a professional working in his or her service, he or she is at definite risk. If the agency has a weak producer and the creatives are dictating specifications or making them up as they go along, the proceedings may well take on the aspects of a Kafka novel.

Orson Welles once described the movie studio as "the greatest train set in the world." Perhaps with that in mind, many agencies are so frightened by the prospect of their own creatives' approaching the process like kids locked in a candy store they do not consider cost plus fixed fee to be a viable option. Agency management knows that cost plus fixed fee requires a fully staffed agency, a strong and skilled production department and one capable of staying atop the job before, during and after the production (something many of them have made difficult by downsizing).

Even with full staffing, detailing expenses on a per job basis is enormously time-consuming and costs difficult to read. If work is underway for several clients simultaneously inside the same production company, all elements are being bought in quantity at the same time, and costs must be apportioned among the clients. The possibility exists that several clients may be furnished the same bills, supported by vendor invoices and everyone overcharged in the process.

The agency producer or business manager must carefully separate and match invoices and examine them against materials actually required and used: how much lumber, how much paint, how much equipment, how many feet of negative. By buying in quantity, discounts accrue to the production house, and these discounts may or may not be reflected in the invoices.

Since final bills are often not examined until months have elapsed and the producer has by now worked on several other jobs, his or her memory of what transpired is cloudy at best. The production company itself is months away from the specifics of the job and must reconstruct events as best they can.

Auditing is a labor-intensive business, and additional costs are exacted by the production company to roll back its tapes and put someone at the agency or client's disposal to answer questions.

For all these reasons, cost plus fixed fee, which should be the most efficient way to work, is largely avoided. Competitive bidding and, indeed, the firm bid process itself is the system preferred by most agencies, most clients and most consultants. Let's consider the firm bid and a few recommended steps for you, the client. It is important that:

1. The agency bid directors and companies comparable in stature and capability.

2. All directors and companies be given the same specifications and time schedules and creative and production units provide equal access and availability.

3. All production companies are bid simultaneously and given equal time to develop bids.

4. All production companies have a legitimate chance to get the job, based on their costs and creative input.

Many production companies complain of being bid only on a check-bid basis, that is the agency has already picked its favorite and is using the others only to show that the preferred bidder is comparable in costs. Bidding takes time and generates costs inside every production company. It is unfair and unprofessional for production houses to be forced to submit to this exercise, particularly if the agency has an in-house production facility that is also included in the bidding. Many production companies are refusing to participate if this is the case or to insist on payment for generating a bid. None of this is necessary if the client has professional assistance, the agency provides a qualified producer and proper use is made of the agency's in-house estimator.

Another legitimate complaint of production houses is that the agency creatives pick the brains of their directors and craftsmen and then selectively feed this information back to their preferred candidate. In effect, this helps sharpen the specifications on an after-the-fact basis, refines the creative approach and negates the competitive bid situation. This is happening with disturbing frequency and may be detected by a close examination of the bids.

The key here is intent. If and when specs are refined, the director and company originating the best thinking should be awarded the job. Of course, such refinement will inevitably color thinking and help the agency in its negotiations with everyone. The issue is one of basic honesty as well as intent.

Production companies are more and more at the mercy of the agencies, especially in the firm bid situation. Stories of rigged bids, favoritism and endless demands made for production work to be done free to help sell the client and the job's then being awarded to another production company are rife within the industry. With fewer commercials being made and competition keen, many production companies are disappearing, victims of high-powered creative groups and high-priced directors whose salaries cause clients and agencies to nickel and dime the rest of the production area to make such directors "more affordable."

Some production companies find their profit margins largely eroded by agencies and clients who keep demanding that more and more be purchased at production house expense as a reward for having been selected from the competition. In the words of one production company manager, "Sometimes I don't know if we've been awarded the job or simply been taken hostage."

The client can, at least to some degree, ameliorate this situation by scrupulously examining bids, insisting that the low bidder be awarded the job and being accessible to production companies with a legitimate grievance.

Picking copy that does not depend for its success on a star director helps widen the opportunities for cost control and supports competition even in such a closed universe as commercial production.

15

Overscale Talent and Print Models

The use of celebrities in advertising is a time-honored tradition. Deals used to be sealed with a handshake after lunch. Things are considerably more complex these days. Entire advertising budgets may be overturned by the inclusion of celebrity or overscale talent.

When the agency suggests the desirability of celebrity talent, the appropriate question to ask is: "What value does this overscale talent bring to the advertising and its memorability, persuasion and believability, and will this translate into additional sales comparable to what the talent is being paid?"

The client is well advised to make use of celebrity rating services independent of the agency to determine who is and who is not widely recognized by the public and the association that talent has. New York City agencies are frequently confounded by their own media hype and insularity. Bobby Short, for instance, is a well-known face and personality to those familiar with the Hotel Carlyle. He may not be so familiar with viewers in Des Moines or even Queens, for that matter. There are also risks in using celebrity talent. Their personal behavior and idiosyncrasies may put the advertiser at risk of unwanted publicity.

Unfortunately, celebrity talent is often used in lieu of a strong selling idea. Cybill Shepherd for L'Oreal is probably a good idea; Cybill Shepherd for the American Beef Council probably is not. Tip O'Neill and Alexander Haig for the Trump shuttle are classic examples of borrowed interest. It is the matchup of comparability, presenter and product that is the key here—how much one personifies the other and/or appears to be a knowing and selective user and endorser of the product.

Seldom is any one celebrity the only choice for a product—often the way that agencies position celebrities to their clients. This precludes any chance for skillful negotiation among a number of suitable candidates. Agencies that routinely contact a celebrity's agent in advance about *their* dollar demands to appear in a client's advertising should be drawn and quartered and then fired—in that order.

Negotiation is always possible. Inside the Hollywood jungle, who is in contention for what advertiser is almost immediately known, and other celebrities' agents will contact agencies to ask to be considered. This sets the stage for sharp negotiations in the client's behalf. One Hollywood glamour queen recently set her asking price for commercial involvement at $750,000. Skillful client negotiations brought that figure down to $75,000 for the first year, with additional sums to accelerate in years 2 and 3. The chances of using the star beyond year 1 are remote. This, by definition, is what negotiating is all about. Sufficient time to negotiate, sufficient candidates from whom to choose and a carefully orchestrated contract are the keys to making the use of celebrity talent pay out.

The options spelled out by the contract are all important. Care must be taken to stage the contract in various periods with payment escalating over time and with sufficient bailout provisions for the agency and client. Traditionally, test usage, regional use, and then national use are standard contract provisions. The rights of usage must also be spelled out, what medium, for how long, as well as associated marketing opportunities: packaging, sales meetings, personal and press appearances, point of purchase and others.

Specifically spelled out should be celebrity availability—when, where, with what notice. These should be under client control as much as possible to avoid crash production schedules driven by celebrity timetables.

The agency should build in restrictions and exclusivity and limitations on appearances in competing categories. You don't want your celebrity touting your diet soft drink and then turning up in an advertisement for a weight reduction regimen.

If you develop a character—Rosie, Mr. Whipple, Madge—the client must make sure he or she owns the character and the costume associated with the character and it cannot be used without permission.

You should be at pains to avoid any creative decision making by the celebrity, particularly the ability to approve copy. Creative input should always be welcomed but never creative control. Similarly, talent should have no voice in selection of programming, magazines where advertising is to appear or choices of director or production company.

Avoid paying for a celebrity's entourage: managers, assistants, hairdressers, makeup artists. They are nearly always overpriced and can increase your budget dramatically by being flown here and there, chauffeured, lodged and fed at plushy rates and then commanding considerable rates for their services.

Also avoid paying the talent agent's commission. This is a 15 percent figure, which should be deducted by the agent from the dollars received, not an additional payment placed atop talent compensation.

Many contracts are hurriedly drawn or are still being negotiated as the talent appears before camera. This usually results in the agent's demanding and getting higher dollar amounts and triple-scale payments applied against the guarantee. If the commercial runs with any frequency, and of course it will, additional payments may have to be made.

Pension and welfare payments should be made by the agency in the client's behalf rather than the star's corporation. This will avoid late payments or non-payments that can generate union penalties and fines.

As you can see, negotiations with celebrity talent require specially trained negotiators inside the agency and increasingly working in behalf of the client with the agency. In spelling out terms and conditions, a talent buy sheet should be used in preliminary and ongoing negotiations. This will also serve later as a cover sheet for the contract and a quick reference for the client.

A talent buy sheet is provided for your examination (see Exhibit 15.1). A sample overscale contract follows (see Exhibit 15.2). This contract should become the principal document used in securing talent services.

Overscale models generally associated with print are being used with increasing frequency by clients in television advertising. Advertisers should be warned of the costs and the risks.

Exhibit 15.1
Talent Buy Sheet

<u>SECTION A</u>   <u>SECTION B</u>

Client:_____

Address:_____

Product:_____

Account Group Contact:_____

Creative Group Contact:_____

Name of Talent whose services are requested:
_____

                               Agent's Name: _____

                               Agent's Address:_____

                                               _____

                               Mailing Address _____
                               for Talent:
                                               _____

        Is Talent operating through a   _____
        corporation or partnership? If a
        corporation, what is the State of
        incorporation. Please provide the
        exact name and address of the entity: _____

        Federal Identification Number: _____

        Talent's Social Security Number: _____
        (Both numbers are required)

TV Commercial(s): No._____ Length_____ _____

  Shoot days required: _____   _____

  Proposed Date(s) of performance:_____   _____

  Proposed Place of performance:_____   _____

Exhibit 15.1 (continued)

Term of Use (from shoot date,
use date or fixed date?)_____   _____

Test Term(s)?
If so, provide details_____   _____

                       _____   _____

                       _____   _____

                       _____   _____

Does the client wish to be able to
extend the right to use the commercial after Term?
If so, for how long?_____   _____

Radio Commercial(s): No._____ Length_____   _____

 Recording days required:_____   _____

 Proposed Date(s) of performance:_____   _____

 Proposed Place of performance:_____   _____

 Term of Use (from shoot date,
 use date or fixed date)_____   _____

 Test Term(s)?
If so, provide details:_____   _____

                       _____   _____

                       _____   _____

                       _____   _____

Does the client wish to be able to
extend the right to use the radio commercial(s)
after the Term?
If so, for how long?_____   _____

Exhibit 15.1 (continued)

Print Advertising
Magazine(s):

Shoot days required:_____   _____

Date(s):_____   _____

Place:_____   _____

Terms of Use:_____   _____
(from shoot date, use
date, or fixed date)_____   _____

Test Term(s)?
If so, provide details:_____   _____

_____   _____

_____   _____

Does the client wish to be able to extend
the right to use the photos after the Term?
If so, for how long:_____   _____

Newspaper(s):

Shoot days required:_____   _____

Date(s):_____   _____

Place:_____   _____

Term of Use: _____   _____
(from shoot date, use
date, or fixed date)_____   _____

Test Term(s)?
If so, provide details:_____   _____

_____   _____

_____   _____

Does the client wish to be able to extend
the right to use the photos after the Term?
If so, for how long?_____   _____

Exhibit 15.1 (continued)

POP/FSI

    Shoot days required:_____   _____

    Date(s):_____   _____

    Place:_____   _____

Term of Use: _____   _____
(from shoot date, use
date, or fixed date)_____   _____

Test Term(s)?
If so, provide details:_____   _____

    _____   _____

    _____   _____

Does the client wish to be able to extend
the right to use the photos after the Term?
If so, for how long?_____   _____

Outdoor Advertising:

    Shoot days required: _____   _____

    Date(s):_____   _____

    Place:_____   _____

Term of Use:_____   _____
(from shoot date, use
date, or fixed date)_____   _____

Test Term(s)?
If so, provide details:_____   _____

    _____   _____

    _____   _____

Does the client wish to be able to extend
the right to use the outdoor boards after the Term?
If so, for how long?_____   _____

Exhibit 15.1 (continued)

PERSONAL APPEARANCE(S):

Date:_____   _____

Place:_____   _____

Duties:_____   _____

Compensation Budget Guidelines   Compensation
If Any

TELEVISION   TELEVISION

Term: $_____   Term: Guarantee of $_____ to
                                                  be applied at _____
Option Term: $_____   times scale.

Test Term(s): $_____   Option Term: Guarantee of $_____
                                                  to be applied at _____
                                                  times scale.

RADIO   RADIO

Term: $_____   Term: Guarantee of $_____ to
be
                                                  applied at _____ times
Option Term: $_____   scale.
                                         Option Term: Guarantee cf $_____ to
Test Term: $_____   be applied at _____
                                                  times scale.

                                         PRINT ADVERTISING:

MAGAZINE(S):   MAGAZINE(S):

Term: $_____   Term: $_____ per photography day

Option Term: $_____   Use Fee: $_____

Test Term: $_____   Option Term(s):_____ per photography
                                                  day

                                         Use Fee: $_____

88

Exhibit 15.1 (continued)

NEWSPAPER(S):

Term: $_____

Option Term: $_____

Test Term: $_____

NEWSPAPER(S):

Term: $_____ per photography day

Use Fee: $_____ per photography day

Option Term(s): $_____ per photography day

Use Fee: $_____

POP/FSI:

Term: $_____

Option Term: $_____

Test Term: $_____

POP/FSI:

Term: $_____ per photography day

Use Fee: $_____ per photography day

Option Term(s): $_____ per photography day

Use Fee: $_____

OUTDOOR:

Term: $_____

Option Term: $_____

Test Term: $_____

OUTDOOR:

Term: $_____ per photography day

Use Fee: $_____ per photography day

Option Term(s): $_____ per photography day

Use Fee: $_____

Travel Expense:

First class round trip air tickets from _____ to _____.

Hotel: Suites_____ Hotel Room_____

Limousine: _____

When is payment required to be made under each of the above categories?

_____   _____

_____   _____

_____   _____

Exhibit 15.1 (continued)

<u>Creative Control</u>: Gillette agrees to give the Talent input into the script, but does <u>not</u> allow talent final script approval. Is this your understanding?

_____   _____

_____   _____

<u>Exclusivity</u>: Do you wish to restrict the products/categories that the Talent can promote during the term of the agreement? If so, list competitive products/categories:

_____   _____

_____   _____

_____   _____

<u>Wardrobe</u>: Is Talent to provide wardrobe? At whose expense? Provide details:

_____   _____

_____   _____

_____   _____

<u>Travel Expenses</u>: Will Talent's travel and out of pocket expenses be paid? Provide details:

_____   _____

_____   _____

_____   _____

<u>OTHER TERMS</u>:   <u>OTHER TERMS</u>:

_____   _____

_____   _____

_____   _____

Exhibit 15.2
Sample Overscale Contract

Date
Name
Street
City,State

Dear:

This letter contains the agreement entered into between
(Talent or Agent as Agent of Talent) and (Company or
Advertising Agency as Agent for Company) concerning your
(client's) appearance in (Company) advertising.

I. SERVICES

    A. INITIAL COMMERCIALS AND TEST PERIOD

You agree to render your services in the making of (number)
(length) television commercials in (place) on (dates) or
such other dates as may be mutually agreed upon. We shall
have the right for three months to make such off-air tests
of each commercial as we choose, and to make two on-air
tests of each commercial, each test to be in not more than
five cities, excluding New York, Chicago and Los Angeles.
If we require your services for a reshooting of said commercials
during the Test Period, you agree to be available for a maximum
of one two-day session for this purpose.

    B. LIMITED USE PERIOD

We shall have the right upon notice to you during the Test
Period to use any commercials made hereunder over any
station or stations in markets representing no more than 33%
of the population of the United States ("Limited Use
Period"). Such Limited Use Period shall be _____
starting with the first such use, subject to our right to
terminate this agreement at the end of the first nine months
of the Limited Use Period or at the end of the next
consecutive six month period of the Limited Use Period upon
30 day notice to you.

    C. UNLIMITED USE PERIOD

We shall have the right upon notice to you either at the end
of the Test Period or during the Limited Use Period to use
the commercials on an unlimited basis over any station or
stations throughout the world ("Unlimited Use Period"). The
term of such Unlimited Use Period shall be _____
starting with the first such use but not later than the end
of the Limited Use Period subject to our right to terminate
this agreement at the end of each consecutive six month
period thereof upon 30 day prior notice to you.

Exhibit 15.2 (continued)

D. <u>TELEVISION COMMERCIALS</u>

We shall have the right to require your services in the
making of such number of additional television commercials
as we may require, or the revision of any commercials
previously made under this agreement, for use during the
Limited Use Period and the Unlimited Use Period. We shall
also have the right to make such number of modifications and
variations of all commercials as we elect by editing, adding
or subtracting from and integrating, without requiring your
additional services, for use during the Limited Time Use
Period and the Unlimited Use Period. If the commercial is to
be dubbed, we shall so inform you.

E. <u>RADIO</u>

We shall have the right to require your services in the
making or revision of such number of radio commercials as we
may require for use during the Limited Use Period and the
Unlimited Use Period in the same manner as TV commercial use
in Paragraphs 1B and 1C.

F. <u>PRINT</u> (in addition to television)

During each of the Limited Use Periods for the United States
and the Unlimited Use Period for the world, we shall have
the right to use your name, voice and likeness, biographical
material and/or signature for advertising, promotion, and
merchandising purposes in and connection with any print
media, including but not limited to, magazines, newspapers,
point-of-purchase, coupons, outdoor billboards, and
transportation advertising. We may use for such purposes
your likeness and/or voice reproduced from any commercials
made hereunder as well as photographs and/or recordings made
expressly for such purposes. Should we require your services
in order to make such photographs or recordings, you agree
to be available to us for such purposes for one one-day
session in the first nine months of the Limited Use Period
and one one-day session each successive six-month period hereof.

* <u>PRINT</u> (alone)

We shall have the right to require your services as a model
at a _____day photographic session on _____.

We shall have the right to reproduce in any manner
whatsoever, in any country in the world, photographs or
other reproductions obtained from the above session, for
advertising, promotion and merchandising purposes in and in
connection with any print media including but not limited to
magazines, newspapers, point-of-purchase, coupons, outdoor
billboards and transportation advertising.

Exhibit 15.2 (continued)

II. <u>COMPENSATION</u>

Subject to the exercise of our options and our termination
rights pursuant to Paragraphs 1B and 1C hereof, we shall
pay you the sum or sums as set forth below:

A. <u>Guarantees</u>

(1) <u>Test Period</u>

$_____ for the three-month period.

(2) <u>Limited Use Period</u>

$ _____for the first nine-month period;

_____for each six-month period of the next
succeeding twelve-month period.

(3). <u>Unlimited Use Period</u>

$_____for each of the first and second six-month
periods;

$_____for each of the third and fourth six-month
periods.

$_____for each of the fifth and six-month periods.

B. <u>TELEVISION COMMERCIALS</u>

A guarantee of $_____for each filming day for which we
require your services.

C. <u>RADIO</u>

A guarantee of $_____for each recording day for which
we require your services.

D. <u>PRINT</u>

(1) $_____for each photographic session for which we
require your services if such session is on a day other than
a commercial filming day.

(2) $_____if we choose to exercise our rights pursuant
to paragraph 1F hereof for use in newspapers, magazines
and coupons, such amount to institute payment for 24 months
starting with the date of the first such use, and, at our
option, $_____for an additional 24 months use.

Exhibit 15.2 (continued)

(3) $_____if we choose to exercise our rights pursuant to paragraph 1F hereof for use in point-of-purchase and in-store display, such amount to constitute payment for 24 months starting with the use of the first such use, and, at our option, $_____for an additional 24 month use.

(4) $_____if we choose to exercise our rights pursuant to paragraph 1F hereof for use in outdoor billboards and transportation advertising, such amount to constitute payment for 24 months starting with the date of the first use, and, at our option, $_____for an additional 24 month use.

E. CREDITING OF GUARANTEES

All guaranteed sums shall be creditable as provided below against all sums due you for television and/or radio commercials at _____times the applicable union scale rate for reuse. Each guaranteed sum paid you is creditable against sums due during the period for which paid, except that after the first nine months of the Limited Use Period and during the Unlimited Use Period the total of the guaranteed sums paid for each twelve-month period shall be creditable against all sums due for such twelve-month period.

Any fees due you which are in excess of the applicable sum to be credited during any period hereunder shall be paid to you within 30 days from the end of the period for which due.

F. TRAVEL AND EXPENSES

Should we require your services outside the area at which you then are, we shall provide you with first class transportation to and from the location at which your services are required, plus hotel accommodations. We shall also pay you $100 for expenses for each day you are required to be at such location.

All sums payable to you hereunder shall be paid to you within ten business days from the date each becomes due except as otherwise expressly provided for hereunder.

Except for any sums which may be due you pursuant to Sub-Paragraphs 2E and F hereof, the applicable guaranteed sums paid you pursuant to Sub-Paragraph 2A hereof shall be deemed full and complete consideration to you for the services rendered by you and for all rights granted to us hereunder.

Exhibit 15.2 (continued)

III. <u>GENERAL PROVISIONS</u>

A. <u>PROMOTION AND PUBLICITY</u>

At any time during the term of this agreement, we shall have the right, at no additional cost to us, to use your name, voice, likeness, biographical material and/or signature either as yourself or as any character you may portray under this agreement, for advertising and publicizing your services in media directed to the trade and in the annual report and internal publications of the (Company), as well as the right to use and distribute Commercial photographs and print advertising reproductions among the marketing and sales personnel of the (Company) as promotional material for the advertising campaign.

B. <u>EXCLUSIVITY</u>

You warrant and represent that you have not participated in or permitted the use of your name, voice or likeness in advertising or promotion for products competitive to this product category, which advertising or promotion may be used during the term of this agreement, and you agree that you will not enter into any such arrangements during the period of time we are permitted to use the commercials and other advertising material, if any, produced under this agreement. However, you may appear in television or radio programs which are sponsored by competitive products, provided you do not appear in any commercial portion of such programs, including billboards, lead-ins to or lead-outs from such commercial portions.

You further warrant and represent that you have not rendered services of any kind as a continuing character in commercials or other advertising for any advertiser whatsoever which may be used during the term of this agreement, and you agree that you will not enter into any such arrangements during the period of time we are permitted to use the commercials and other advertising material, if any, produced under this agreement.

C. <u>CALLS</u>

We shall give you reasonable advance notice of all dates on which we require you to render services, provided, however, we shall not have the right to require you to render services on a date which will conflict with a bona fide performance commitment which you may have made prior to receiving notice from us that your services are to be rendered on such date. In the event of such conflict, you will advise us of the soonest possible date on which you can render services hereunder without such rendition conflicting with a bona fide performance commitment, it being understood that it is the intent of this agreement that you be reasonably available to render the services required of you hereunder.

Exhibit 15.2 (continued)

D. SERVICE

You agree to render all of your services hereunder in a
competent, painstaking and artistic manner, to the best of
your ability and in accordance with the script and other
material or direction which we furnish to you. Your services
shall be subject to our approval, direction and control at
all times. You will attend and participate in all rehearsals,
conferences and such other meetings that we shall deem
necessary or advisable in connection with the rendition of
your services hereunder.

E. DELAYED BROADCAST

We shall have the right to broadcast any commercials made
hereunder for a period not to exceed 30 days immediately
following the termination of expiration of our right to use
said commercials, solely in connection with the delayed
broadcast in any market of a program containing any such
commercial which program shall have been broadcast on the
network prior to the termination or expiration of such
rights.

F. RIGHTS TO ADVERTISING MATERIALS

You agree that any commercials or other advertising
materials produced under this agreement, including all
elements thereof, shall be and remain the absolute property
of (Company) forever provided that our use of any such
advertising material beyond the term of this agreement shall
not include the right to use your name, voice, and/or
likeness as a part thereof except for such point-of-purchase
or trade materials which may have been distributed or
produced for distribution prior to the termination or
expiration of this agreement. You agree that you will not
claim to have, either under this agreement or otherwise, any
right, title or interest of any kind or nature whatsoever in
and to any commercials or other advertising materials
produced hereunder.

G. INSURANCE

We shall have the right to insure your life on behalf of
(Company) and you will cooperate with us in obtaining such
insurance.

H. BREACH

If you at any time should breach any provision of this
agreement, or at any time fail, neglect or refuse to fulfill
any of your obligations hereunder, then we shall have the
right, in addition to our other legal and equitable
remedies, to terminate this agreement forthwith and the
guaranteed sum paid to you for the period in which such
termination occurs shall be refunded to us by you on a
pro-rata basis.

Exhibit 15.2 (continued)

I. <u>MORALS</u>

During the term hereof, you agree to conduct yourself at all times with due regard to public morals and conventions. If you shall have committed or shall commit any act or do anything that is or shall be an offense involving moral turpitude under federal, state or local laws, or which tends to bring you into public disrepute, contempt, scandal or ridicule, or which tends to insult or offend the community, or which shall injure the success of (Company) or any of (Company) products, then at the time of any such act or at any time after we learn of any such act, we shall have the right, in addition to our other legal and equitable remedies, to terminate this agreement forthwith and the guaranteed sum paid to you for the period in which such termination occurs shall be refunded to us on a pro-rata basis.

J. <u>INABILITY TO RENDER SERVICES</u>

If for any reason during the term hereof, including death, disfigurement or physical or mental disability, you become unable to render the services provided for herein, then we shall have the right, in addition to our other legal and equitable remedies, to terminate this agreement forthwith and the guaranteed sum paid to you for the period in which such termination occurs shall be refunded to us on a pro-rata basis.

K. <u>UNION COMPLIANCE</u>

You agree that during the term of this agreement, you will be and remain a member in good standing of the Screen Actor's Guild, AFTRA, and any other union having lawful jurisdiction over the performance of the services to be performed by you under this agreement. This agreement shall be subject to and we and (Company) shall be entitled to all benefits applicable to producers or sponsors under all appropriate union agreements or codes.

L. <u>WARRANTY</u>

You represent and warrant that you have the right and power to enter into and perform this agreement without violating the legal or equitable rights of anyone.

M. <u>EQUITABLE RIGHTS</u>

It is mutually agreed that your services are special, unique unusual, extraordinary and of an artistic character, giving them a peculiar value, and are impossible of replacement and that any breach of this agreement by you will cause (Company) irreparable damage. You, therefore, agree that we and (Company) shall be entitled as a matter of right, and without notice, to equitable relief by way of injunction or otherwise in the event of any violation of the provisions of this agreement.

Exhibit 15.2 (continued)

N. COMMISSIONS

You agree that we shall be under no obligation for the payment of any commissions on account of this agreement.

O. PAY OR PLAY

You agree that we shall be under no obligation to use any commercials or other advertising materials made hereunder or to make use of your services, it being understood that our only obligation is to make payments to you in accordance with the terms hereof.

P. INDEMNIFICATION

You agree to indemnify and hold harmless us, (Company), and their and our respective directors, agents, licensees, employees, successors and assigns from and against any and all claims (a) arising out of any breach by you of any understanding, warranty, representation or agreement contained herein or (b) arising out of the proper exercise by us of rights granted by you to us hereunder. We agree to similarly indemnify you with respect to material furnished by us to you.

Q. WAIVER

The failure of any party hereto to exercise the rights granted them herein upon the occurrence of any of the contingencies set forth in this agreement shall not in any event constitute a waiver of any such rights upon the recurrence of any such contingencies.

R. NOTICES

Any notice to be given by us to you hereunder shall be deemed to have been sufficiently given if delivered personally or by mail to you at your address stated above; and if the notice is to be given to us, then by your forwarding notice in the same manner to us at our address stated above. Any notice so mailed shall be deemed to have been given on the day it is mailed.

S. ENTIRE UNDERSTANDING

This agreement constitutes the entire understanding between you and us with regard to the subject matter covered herein and shall supersede and replace any and all other agreements, whether written or oral. No waiver, modification, or addition to this agreement shall be valid unless in writing and signed by an authorized representative of the party or parties to be affected.

Exhibit 15.2 (continued)

T. APPLICABLE LAW

This agreement and all matters or issues collateral thereto
shall be governed by the laws of the Commonwealth of
_____ applicable to contracts made and performed
entirely within.

Your signature at the end hereof, together with ours, shall
constitute this a full and binding agreement.

Very truly yours,

(Company or Agency as Agent for Company)

_____

Accepted and Agreed to:

By _____

Date _____

Affirmed:

By _____
            (talent)

Date_____

Advertising agencies have done a remarkably poor job of controlling print models in the areas of working contracts and costs. The result has been paying print day rates for television—$5,000 and up per day and usually more—with payments of agents' fees over and above their salaries (an unheard-of practice outside this area).

Many seasoned print models are a delight to work with and have professional aspirations for moving into the movies; more than a few young, overnight sensations, however, have let their newfound success go to their heads. The result is that, they show little or no allegiance to schedules, clients or their own agencies. Many agree to conflicting schedules, conflicting clients and competitive products with no reservation, before or after the fact. Several advertisers have been stung by the same model's showing up in several of their competitors' television commercials and print ads running simultaneously and in the same product category.

Some have been known not to show up at a shooting and since they are not members of SAG/AFTRA (Screen Actors Guild/American Federation of Television, Radio Artists) or bound by union regulations, they are considered free agents. Consequently, a costly shooting might fold because the model has "forgotten" to show up or received a better offer only the night before. His or her agency will express regrets and commiserate but make no mention of who pays for the scrapped day or the hurried attempts to recast. The agency will simply tell you there will be no charge for the model's services, since she or he didn't show up.

If you decide to use an overscale print model for television, have a contract drawn in advance that places the cost of the production day on the model's agency as well as on the model should he or she not arrive for the day. Insist on exclusivity in your specific product category, and make it known to the agency in advance that any prior appearance in the same category should be revealed to the agency or client in advance and any agreement not to appear in competitive advertising in the same category will be enforced. Vigorously pursue the agency or model if this should occur with whatever legal means are at your disposal. What you will find as the issue of exclusivity is pursued is that both the model and agency will be surprised at your seriousness in this area. You will then be asked to pay a daunting sum for the privilege. For any of the well-known faces, the going rate is about $1 million and up.

Keep all this in mind when your eye falls on some magazine page in the future, and there, smiling out at you, is a young dazzler, fresh faced and lithesome, who you know would be just right for your next television commercial. Their own agents refer to them as smiling sharks. Swim at your own risk.

16

The AICP Form

The Association of Independent Commercial Producers is a national trade association representing eighty percent of all commercial production companies in the United States. It has become an important presence in setting industry bidding procedures and standards.

Prior to the standardization of the AICP form as the lingua franca of commercial production, every production company, every agency and many clients had their own bid forms. This made the reading of comparative bids a difficult and time-consuming practice. The successful implementation of the AICP form industrywide has provided a genuine service and has led to the origination of a similar form for editorial services.

Here for your inspection is the AICP Film Production Bid Form (see Exhibit 16.1). (The AICP Videotape Production Cost Summary appears as Appendix A and the AICP Glossary appears as Appendix B.) The AICP form breaks out all costs in the job on an item-by-item basis.

In the case of a firm bid, the Estimated cost is the only column to be filled in, since the price quoted is regarded as the final actual cost. In the case of cost plus fixed fee, Estimated versus Actual will reflect the differences between what has been planned and the actual costs of the production as validated by invoices.

The top Summary page carries forward all cost information and groups it. These are understood to be direct costs paid by the production company without markup and totaled on line 9. The Pro-

Exhibit 16.1
Film Production Cost Summary

	FIRM BID
	COST PLUS

			Bid Date	Actualization Date

Production Co.:		Agency:	Agency job #
Address:		Client:	Product:
Telephone No.:	Job #		
Production Contact:		Agency prod:	Tel:
Director:		Agency art dir:	Tel;
Cameraman:		Agency writer:	Tel:
Set Designer:		Agency Bus. Mgr.:	Tel:
Editor:		Commercial title:	No.: Length:
No. pre-prod. days	pre-light/rehearse	1.	
No. build/strike days	Hours:	2.	
No. Studio shoot days	Hours:	3.	
No. Location days	Hours:	4.	
Location sites:		5.	
		6.	

SUMMARY OF ESTIMATED PRODUCTION COSTS		ESTIMATED	ACTUAL		
1. Pre-production and wrap costs	Totals A & C				
2. Shooting crew labor	Total B				
3. Location and travel expenses	Total D				
4. Props, wardrobe, animals	Total E				
5. Studio & Set Construction Costs	Totals F, G, and H				
6. Equipment costs	Total I				
7. Film stock develop and print: No. feet mm	Total J				
8. Miscellaneous	Total K				
9.	Sub-Total: A to K				
10. Director/creative fees (Not Included In Direct Cost)	Total L				
11. Insurance					
12.	Sub-Total: Direct Costs				
13. Production Fee					
14. Talent costs and expenses	Totals M and N				
15. Editorial and finishing per:					
16.					
17.	Grand Total (Including Director's Fee)				
18. Contingency					

Comments:

Exhibit 16.1 (continued)

	CREW	A: PRE-PRO/WRAP										B: SHOOT								
		ESTIMATED				ACTUAL						ESTIMATED				ACTUAL			
		Days	Rate	O/T Hrs	Total	Days	Rate	O/T $	Total			Days	Rate	O/T Hrs	Total	Days	Rate	O/T $	Total
1	Producer:									51									
2	Assistant Director:									52									
3	Director Photography:									53									
4	Camera Operator:									54									
5	Asst. Cameraman:									55									
6	Outside Prop:									56									
7										57									
8	Inside Prop:									58									
9										59									
10										60									
11	Electrician:									61									
12										62									
13										63									
14										64									
15										65									
16	Grip:									66									
17										67									
18										68									
19										69									
20	Mixer:									70									
21	Boom Man:									71									
22	Recordist:									72									
23	Playback:									73									
24	Make-Up:									74									
25	Hair:									75									
26	Stylist:									76									
27	Wardrobe Attendant:									77									
28	Script Clerk:									78									
29	Home Economist:									79									
30	Asst. Home Economist:									80									
31	VTR Man:									81									
32	EFX Man:									82									
33	Scenic:									83									
34	Telepr. Operator:									84									
35	Generator Man:									85									
36	Still Man:									86									
37	Loc. Contact/Scout:									87									
38	P.A.									88									
39	2nd A.D.									89									
40	Nurse:									90									
41	Craft Service:									91									
42	Fireman:									92									
43	Policeman:									93									
44	Wlfr./Tchr.:									94									
45	Teamster									95									
46										96									
47										97									
48										98									
49										99									
50										100									
		Sub Total A										Sub Total B								
		PT/P & W										PT/P & W								
		TOTAL A										TOTAL B								

Exhibit 16.1 (continued)

PRE-PRODUCTION & WRAP/MATERIALS & EXPENSES	ESTIMATED	ACTUAL	
101. Auto Rentals (No. of Cars)			
102. Air Fares: No. of people ( ) x Amount per fare ( )			
103. Per Diems: No. of people ( ) x Amount per day ( )			
104. Still Camera Rental & Film			
105. Messengers			
106. Trucking			
107. Deliveries & Taxis			
108. Home Economist Supplies			
109. Telephone & Cable			
110. Casting Call/Prep_____ Days Casting _____ Days Call Back _____ Days			
111. Casting Facilities			
112. Working Meals			
113.			
Sub Total C			

LOCATION EXPENSES	ESTIMATED	ACTUAL	
114. Location Fees			
115. Permits			
116. Car Rentals			
117. Bus Rentals			
118. Camper Dressing Room Vehicles			
119. Parking, Tolls, & Gas			
120. Trucking			
121. Other vehicles			
122. Other vehicles			
123. Customs			
124. Air freight/ Excess baggage			
125. Air Fares: No. of people ( ) x cost per fare ( )			
126. Per Diems: Total No. man days ( ) x amt. per day ( )			
127. Air fares: No. of people ( ) x cost per fare ( )			
128. Per Diems: Total No. man days ( ) x amt. per day ( )			
129. Breakfast: No. of man days ( ) x amt. per person ( )			
130. Lunch: No. of man days ( ) x amt. per person ( )			
131. Dinner: No. of man days ( ) x amt. per person ( )			
132. Guards			
133. Limousines (Celebrity Service)			
134. Cabs and Other Transportation			
135. Kit Rental			
136. Art Work			
137. Gratuities			
138.			
139.			
Sub Total D			

PROPS AND WARDROBE & ANIMALS	ESTIMATED	ACTUAL	
140. Prop Rental			
141. Prop Purchase			
142. Wardrobe Rental			
143. Wardrobe Purchase			
144. Picture Vehicles			
145. Animals & Handlers			
146. Wigs & Mustaches			
147. Color Correction			
148.			
149.			
150.			
Sub Total E			

Exhibit 16.1 (continued)

STUDIO RENTAL & EXPENSES—STAGE	ESTIMATED				ACTUAL			
	Days	Hrs	Rate	Total	Days	Hrs	Rate	Total
151. Rental for Build Days								
152. Rental for Build O.T. Hours								
153. Rental for Pre-Lite Days								
154. Rental for Pre-Lite O.T. Hours								
155. Rental for Shoot Days								
156. Rental for Shoot O.T. Hours								
157. Rental for Strike Days								
158. Rental for Strike O.T. Hours								
159. Generator & Operator								
160. Set Guards								
161. Total Power Charge & Bulbs								
162. Misc. Studio Charges (Cartage, Phone, Coffee)								
163. Meals for Crew & Talent (Lunch, Dinner)								
164.								
165.								
166.								
167.								
Sub Total F								

SET CONSTRUCTION (CREW FOR BUILD, STRIKE, PRELIGHT)	ESTIMATED				ACTUAL			
	Days	Rate	O/T Hrs.	Total	Days	Rate	O/T $	Total
168. Set Designer Name:								
169. Carpenters								
170. Grips								
171. Outside Props								
172. Inside Props								
173. Scenics								
174. Electricians								
175. Teamsters								
176. Men for Strike								
177. P.A.s								
178.								
179.								
180.								
Sub Total G								
PT/P & W								
TOTAL G								

SET CONSTRUCTION MATERIALS	ESTIMATED	ACTUAL	
181. Props (Set Dressing Purchase)			
182. Props (Set Dressing Rental)			
183. Lumber			
184. Paint			
185. Hardware			
186. Special Effects			
187. Special Outside Construction			
188. Trucking			
189. Messengers/Deliveries			
190. Kit Rental			
191.			
192.			
Sub Total H			

Exhibit 16.1 (continued)

EQUIPMENT RENTAL	ESTIMATED	ACTUAL	
193. Camera Rental			
194. Sound Rental			
195. Lighting Rental			
196. Grip Rental			
197. Generator Rental			
198. Crane/Cherry Picker Rental			
199. VTR Rental With Playback _____ Without Playback _____			
200. Walkie Talkies, Bull Horns			
201. Dolly Rental			
202. Camera Car			
203. Helicopter			
204. Production Supplies			
205. Teleprompter			
206.			
207.			
208.			
209.			
210.			
Sub Total I			

FILM RAW STOCK DEVELOP AND PRINT	ESTIMATED			ACTUAL		
	FOOTAGE	COST/FT.	TOTAL	FOOTAGE	COST/FT.	TOTAL
211. Purchase of raw stock: Footage amount						
212. Developing footage amount						
243. Printing footage amount						
214. Transfer to Mag.						
215. Sync/Screen Dailies						
216.						
Sub Total J						

MISCELLANEOUS COSTS	ESTIMATED	ACTUAL	
217. Petty Cash			
218. Air Shipping/Special Carriers			
219. Phones and Cables			
220. Accountable Cash Expenditures Under $15 Each			
221. External Billing Costs (Computer Accounting, etc.)			
222. Special Insurance			
223.			
224.			
225.			
226.			
Sub Total K			

DIRECTOR/CREATIVE FEES	ESTIMATED	ACTUAL	
227. Prep			
228. Travel			
229. Shoot Days			
230. Post-production			
231.			
232.			
233.			
Sub Total L			

Exhibit 16.1 (continued)

TALENT	No.	Rate	Days	TRAVEL DAYS	O/T Hrs 1½ X	2X	ESTIMATED	No.	Days	ACTUAL
234. O/C Principals										
235. O/C Principals										
236. O/C Principals										
237. O/C Principals										
238. O/C Principals										
239. O/C Principals										
240. O/C Principals										
241. O/C Principals										
242. O/C Principals										
243. O/C Principals										
244.										
245.										
246.										
247. General Extras										
248. General Extras										
249. General Extras										
250. General Extras										
251. General Extras										
252. General Extras										
253.										
254.										
255.										
256. Hand Model										
257.										
258.										
259. Voice Over										
260. Fitting Fees: S.A.G.										
261. Fitting Fees: S.E.G.										
262.										
263. Audition Fees: S.A.G.										
264. Audition Fees: S.E.G.										
265.										
Sub Total										
266. Payroll & P&W Taxes										
267. Wardrobe Allowance: No. of talent ( ) x No. of garments ( ) x fee per garment ( ).										
268.										
Sub Total										
269. Other										
270. Mark-up										
Sub Total M										

TALENT EXPENSES	ESTIMATED	ACTUAL	
271. Per diem: No. of man days ( ) x amount per day ( )			
272. Air fare: No. of people ( ) x amount per fare ( )			
273. Cabs and other transportation			
274. Mark-Up			
275.			
276.			
Sub Total N			

duction Fee (line 13) is put atop these costs and represents the production house markup (generally 26 to 35 percent).

Line 10 reflects the director's fee and includes all his or her costs for pre-production and production.

Elements 1–9, A–K, are the areas to which you, the client, should pay closest attention. (You should not be paying markup on insurance.)

Item 14, Talent Costs and Expenses, rarely appears on the production bid, and they should not. The agency should be paying talent directly to avoid the production company markup. The only exception may be the hiring of general extras by the production company.

Item 15, Editorial and Finishing, also rarely appears on the production bid since editorial work is usually farmed out to an editorial company. These figures will be supplied separately (and examined in a later chapter), but editorial and all other costs, including original music or any special casting expenses, should also be reflected in the total bid sent forward for your examination. Moreover, all costs submitted for your reaction should always be gross costs reflecting agency markup since these are the actual complete costs you will be signing off on in your approval for work to commence.

Item 18, Contingency, is in reality the studio's estimate of costs for the weather day (if the shooting is postponed by rain, snow or high winds). This figure should always be carefully negotiated by the agency producer before the fact, as to who pays what and how much. (Qualified producers need no instruction in this area.)

The arrival of the AICP form saw all cost categories broken out in the fullest and most complete manner to date. Some categories included immediately drew attention by their inclusion. In reality, what was happening here was that the AICP was detailing cost elements, some of which had formerly been overlooked or absorbed by production companies and covered by their higher markup rates—40 percent or more—at one time.

In the past, profit margins were a good deal higher and work a good deal more plentiful and constant. Editorial services were part of the parent production company, and overseeing the entire production gave the production facilities greater profitability. All of this changed in the 1970s and 1980s with the arrival of "boutique houses"—usually a star director and a limited staff and separate editorial facilities providing "more personalized service" for agencies and clients. Fewer commercials are also being made each year as advertisers plow more dollars into promotion and trade allowances. All of this, in addition to the enormous changes in technology that have required nearly constant upgrading of facilities and equipment, has put enormous pressures on production companies not only to show a profit but just to stay in business. It is in the face of these industry downturns that the AICP was formed and has grown in importance.

The AICP is not without its critics. The AICP form itself is coming under increasing scrutiny because of the inclusion of a number of categories that many producers and clients feel are questionable or redundant. For example, categories 36, 37 and 104 provide for a Still Man, a Location Contact/Scout and a Still Camera Rental & Film. Usually the location scout is the assistant director, already covered in category 2. The camera most often is a studio-owned Polaroid. Why, then, are there categories for these charges?

Under category 1 a number of "Production Assistants" may be included. These may or may not be personnel already on staff in some lesser capacity. Should the client be paying for people already on staff and presumably covered by the studio's markup? And since these assistants are sent out routinely to run errands, why are there separate charges for Messengers (105), Deliveries & Taxis (107), Cabs and Other Transportation (134) and Messengers/ Deliveries (189)? The same question of intent arises in Auto Rentals secured for Pre-Production/Wrap (101). Since cars are usually rented for the entire shooting, start to finish, why are Car Rentals (116), also found, along with Parking, Tolls, & Gas (119) and Cabs and Other Transportation (134)?

Production companies using the AICP form can provide explanations for all these questions and why they are being treated separately. The question is, Should they be treated separately? Critics of the AICP, and indeed critics of any production form generated by production companies, see these forms as suspect. Only half-jokingly some producers say that there is nothing to prevent future production forms from selling sound stages by the piece, with Walls, Floors and Ceilings shown as three separate cost categories or the invention of new categories, such as shoes worn by the crew being listed as Special Production Footwear.

All of these matters need to be resolved, along with a greater sense of integration between the designers of the form and those who must use it. Such discussions are underway, and there is a growing sense of cooperation between agencies and production companies. It is important that knowledgeable client representatives also be involved in any future discussions. Although the ANA and Procter & Gamble (among others) have importantly contributed here, greater advertiser involvement is necessary to represent the third and perhaps most important member of the triumvirate: the client, who pays the bills.

In assessing bids, you, the client, should understand that the AICP form represents only a buying guide. Costs indicated in every category are subject to question, negotiation and elimination by you and the agency. "Is this element necessary? What is this really buying me? What if I say 'no' to this? Will I see the difference? How? Where? Is there a cheaper way to do this?" These are the kinds of questions you should be posing to the agency on a line-by-line basis about anything you don't understand.

Again, remember, that the agency considers the client largely responsible for controlling costs. This means you need a qualified production representative working with the agency and production company and posing those questions in ways that demand genuine answers and reduced, efficient costs.

Let's explore next how you or your production representative should go about the business of using the AICP form to your advantage.

17

Cutting Costs of the Individual Commercial

It is essential to the success of the advertising that you make use of the agency producer and whatever expertise has been provided for your division and brand in staff support or outside counsel. These experts bring a value to the proceedings well beyond the money saved. Indeed, their first allegiance is and must be with making the advertising translate as successfully as possible onto film.

Each director and production company has looked at the storyboard and the specifications, discussed the work with the agency and elected to make certain creative decisions that are reflected in the bids. One director may decide to put more time into preparation for the job. Another may elect to shoot on location rather than build a set. Another may decide a set is preferable but a smaller set propped more extensively with the camera in closer to be able to detect the small touches provided. All of this is to say that there will be differences reflected between all the bids and their internals based on individual interpretations of how the job should be produced.

Differences aside, a certain amount of consistency in the bidding will be evident because directors and companies are looking at the same storyboard, reading the same specs and have had the same discussions on creative intent and production limitations with the creatives and agency producer. No production company will risk not providing enough dollars in any category to shortchange the production. A careful examination of the bids on a line-by-line basis will provide you with a clear cost range by category. As you will quickly see, the high bidder may be lower in some categories, and the low bidder may be higher in some categories.

Depending on your expertise in the production process, your ability to go through the 276 lines of production information on each bid will give you a detailed blueprint of where dollars are being placed and for what purpose. If your expertise is less than professional in production, you are best served staying with the Summary Page and categories A-K.

Spread the cover pages side by side and review the top lines of the Summary of Estimated Production Costs from each house. On a line-by-line basis, note which amount is lowest in each category. If you add the lowest dollar amount reflected on every sheet on a line-by-line basis, you will arrive at a rough estimate of the lowest cost possible to shoot this commercial as indicated by the suppliers who have bid on the work. This is only the roughest kind of indicator but helpful nonetheless.

Close examination may also help detect variances that you will want to discuss with the agency. For instance, why does one director estimate 3,000 feet of negative and another 5,000? The more negative is exposed, the longer is the shooting day. Does the director whose overall costs show him to be low bidder still have a larger dollar amount reflected in sets and propping? This may indicate he was one of the first directors to be bid and since initial discussions with him, the agency has pulled back slightly in what they are looking for in the area of sets.

Each bid is subject to negotiation and refinement before the job is awarded. This means that more exposition and detail may be given to each production company. Their original figures may be refined and reflect further thinking on the part of the agency, the client and/ or the production company itself.

Let me take you through a recent job I worked on to share some insight as to how production requirements may be refined and how this affects the bottom line. The storyboard under discussion is simple in design. Two bedrooms are seen, one after the other. Each belongs to a teenager. It is night. Both kids talk to camera about the product they are using, and it is seen on the nightstand by their bed. Each scene ends with the lights being turned off and then a close-up shot of the product, accompanied by a super and a voice-over announcer.

The commercial had been sent out for bids by the time the advertiser asked me to participate; specs were set, and the client had not indicated to the agency a prior cost ceiling. The first indication of costs was relayed to the client after bidding began. Preliminary discussions with a New York company indicated gross totals were being estimated somewhere in the range of $200,000 to $225,000. The client reacted with surprise. He had been hoping to spend no more than $130,000 but could go up to $150,000 gross.

I began with the first logical step: examining the board, the specifications and the arrival at a cost ceiling to be given the agency and this figure (belatedly) passed along to all bidders. It was apparent that without substantial reworking of the specifications (and probably the board), there was little likelihood of reducing costs to the client's indicated level.

The first elements that the agency and I discussed and removed were original music, and the pre-light day, and we generally simplified the sets. Costs were reduced some $40,000 in the initial pass. Following are the cost summaries received from the three competing production houses at that stage in the negotiation. Remember that these costs are net amounts and do not reflect costs of editing, stock music or agency commission:

1.	Pre-Pro/Wrap Costs	$16,807	$20,671	$25,970
2.	Shooting/Crew Labor	17,565	15,881	14,211
3.	Location/Travel	———	———	———
4.	Props, Wardrobe	16,950	300	2,050
5.	Studio/Set Construction	33,584	46,519	46,393
6.	Equipment Costs	7,850	10,000	11,450
7.	Film Stock/Dev. Print	4,310	2,705	5,200
8.	Miscellaneous	750	200	850
9.	Subtotal: A–K	97,615	96,276	106,124
10.	Director/Creative Fee	8,750	8,000	8,840
11.	Insurance	2,198	1,926	2,122
12.	Direct Costs	108,651	106,202	117,086
13.	Production Fee	29,284	33,697	37,143
	Grand Total:	$137,846	$139,899	$154,229

Editorial charges were estimated at $12,000 and stock music at $1,100. With an agency commission of 17.65 percent, the gross cost to client ranged from $177,588 to $197,000—still well above the client's intent.

When we scrutinized the costs generated by all those bidding, we found considerable disparity in nearly every category, including how much footage was to be exposed and printed in shooting the commercial. Set costs ranged from $46,393 and $33,584, propping costs from $16,950 to $300, and pre-pro wrap costs from $25,970 to $16,807.

Accordingly we focused on the sets and the amount of building and propping. We decided as a result of these discussions that the second scene, which was short and essentially a reiteration of the first, could be eliminated. Staging the action closer in the one remaining set could reduce demands for sets and props, which in turn would reduce crew time and the amount of footage needed.

The job was then rebid with the highest bidder dropped from contention (he had been awarded another job) and another production company asked to bid. Here is how the information now broke out from the three companies:

1. Pre-Pro/Wrap Costs	$19,250	$15,915	$14,227
2. Shooting/Crew Labor	13,086	15,016	14,984
3. Location/Travel			
4. Props, Wardrobe	150	8,900	3,700
5. Studio/Set Construction	34,309	22,778	30,044
6. Equipment Costs	9,550	6,900	7,950
7. Film Stock/Dev. Print	2,685	4,310	2,997
8. Miscellaneous	200	750	200
9. Subtotal: A–K	79,230	74,568	74,182
10. Director/Creative Fee	8,000	8,675	6,600
11. Insurance	1,585	1,678	
12. Subtotal: Direct Costs	88,815	84,921	80,782
13. Production Fee	27,731	21,625	14,836
Grand Total:	$116,546	$106,546	$95,618

Since the editorial requirements were also simpler, the costs of editing were reduced to $9,300. Stock music was set at $1,100.

The client elected to go with the low bidder. Once costs of editorial and stock music were included, the net cost of the job was $106,018, which grossed up to $124,730. The entire process of negotiation took eight working days and showed a savings of about $52,858.

It is important to note that for every dollar extracted on a line-by-line basis of direct costs, further savings are generated by eliminating extra costs in pension and welfare, taxes, studio markup and agency commission. Thus, for every $1.00 extracted from direct costs, a genuine savings of about $1.64 is realized by the client.

The key to lowering costs is accomplished in a simple, ongoing manner: setting a price for the advertising in advance, simplifying advertising in its internal construction, sharpening specifications and buying only what is needed.

The job is now awarded.

18

Ensuring a Successful Shooting: The Pre-Production Meeting

The purpose of the pre-production meeting and the roles of producer and director may be best understood by a brief exchange between Hollywood's David Selznick, producer, and Alfred Hitchcock, director, as work began on *Rebecca* in 1940. "I hope you're not going to tell me where to put my camera and when to move it," Hitchcock said. "Absolutely not," Selznick replied. "I'm just going to tell you what I want to have up on the screen when you're done."

The purpose of the pre-production meeting for you, the client, is to make sure both the agency and the production company know what you want to have up on the screen when they're done. To accomplish this end, the pre-production meeting is the place to:

1. Review final copy.
2. Time the board for proper playing length.
3. Finalize casting and book talent.
4. Finalize set and wardrobe selection.
5. Direct how product demonstrations are to be conducted and shot.
6. Come to complete agreement on communication takeaway of every scene in the commercial.
7. Establish final timetables and costs.

The pre-production meeting is, or should be, the last discussion of intent. It is the hand-off place where creators of the idea give responsibility for achieving that idea in physical form on film to the director and staff. In reality, this is not so much a giving away of authority as it is an embrace of greater authority in the process of filmmaking thanks to the director's skill and familiarity with the tools of the craft. The essential goal of the pre-production meeting is that everyone involved with the shooting is of one mind. If the meeting has been successfully accomplished, it should be unnecessary for either the client or the agency creatives to attend the actual shooting to control what happens there.

There may be as many as thirty people in a pre-production meeting. This is unfortunate but sometimes necessary. Only decision makers from the client side should attend. The client's production representative should speak for the company as the producer speaks for the agency.

The storyboard should be reviewed, first for words to be sure any last-minute legal changes have been accomplished and recorded. The board should be timed once again to be sure any added or deleted words have not affected the commercial's playing length. Then the board should be reviewed visually scene by scene.

Film is a detail-demanding medium. It does not allow for cloudy thinking or indecision. The camera records only what is put before it. Importance and significance are prompted by how close an object is to camera and how long each shot runs. There is a tempo to film that is as important to film as it is to music.

If there is any question as to intent, clarify it now, scene by scene and shot by shot. If tonality is in question, show a previous commercial example. Rather than inhibit the director, this will provide a visual frame of reference and a point of departure.

Any legal or technical information that is needed must be detailed in writing and completely understood by everyone from the production company. The production house will be expected to provide a legal affidavit testifying to how results were accomplished. This is especially important if any comparative claims are made and any question arises from a competitor as to validity in visual claim.

Forms detailing how demonstrations were accomplished, forms certifying actual product use on camera and details on those who provide testimonials are included here for your inspection (see Exhibits 18.1, 18.2 and 18.3). They are the responsibility of the agency, and copies should be forwarded to clients for their files.

A storyboard provided by the director (called a shooting board) can

Exhibit 18.1
Advertising Production Producer's Affidavit

State of   )

) ss.

County of   )

PRODUCT: _____

COMMERCIAL TITLE:_____

FILM NO: _____

I, _____, hereby state that the following is a true and accurate record

of events:

1. The above –named commercial was produced by _____
                                                           (Production Studio)

   on _____ at _____
                     (Date)   (Address of Studio)

2. I was present for the entire filming of the commercial.

3. _____, the product depicted in the commercial, was obtained as follows:
               (Name of Product)

_____

4. Attached hereto are the specifications for the demonstration depicted in the commercial.

5. Every aspect of the demonstration in the commercial was produced in accordance with said specifications.

6. The filming or taping of this commercial was conducted in a truthful and accurate manner, and no undisclosed

   props or other procedures were employed so as to enhance the results any more favorably than what was

   filmed or taped.

PRODUCER: _____

Sworn to before me this _____ day of

_____, 19___ .

_____
Notary Public

Exhibit 18.2
Advertising Production Certification of Product Use

PRODUCT: _____

COMMERCIAL TITLE: _____

FILM NO: _____

I, _____, hereby certify that

I used _____ within twenty-four hours and in
(Name of Product)

accordance with instructions on the package. I further certify that the product performed as represented in the

above-captioned commercial, filmed on _____
(Date)

at _____
(Address of Studio)

and the results obtained were as depicted in said commercial.

Date: _____   _____
                                    Talent

                                    _____
                                    Agency

be of enormous benefit in showing not only how action is to be staged but the framing of each shot and transitions from scene to scene. All of this will serve to clarify and speed the editorial process later. Hollywood has been storyboarding movies for generations, and the discipline is a good one. No amount of verbalization can accomplish what a single drawing can do.

The director should put time frames against the board: when what is to be shot, in what order and how long that scene should take to accomplish. The hallmark of a good shooting is drive. Successful film builds on momentum in its making and in its final power as a medium.

Alternate scenes or versions should seldom if ever, be allowed. These not only consume time (and dollars) but contribute to a loss of momentum. It may be possible to cover an alternate idea in the announcer soundtrack, and if this is possible, by all means use it. This is especially true if the alternate is meant to accomplish some legal purpose.

The pre-production meeting is the place to discuss, agree and disagree and at last come to a meeting of the minds. The meeting should not end until that has been accomplished. The pre-production meeting is also the most relevant time and place to encourage and explore

Exhibit 18.3
Advertising Production Testimonial Questionnaire

PRODUCT: _____

COMMERCIAL TITLE: _____

FILM NO: _____

NAME OF TESTIFIER: _____

1. How was the testifier contacted and selected?

2. Was the testifier a user of the product or service prior to being contacted by the advertiser or his agency?

3. How long has the testifier been a user of the product or service?

4. To the best of your knowledge and belief is the testifier related to or personally acquainted in private life with any person employed by the advertiser, his agency or other firms in the employ of the advertiser or his agency?

5. To the best of your knowledge and belief has the testifier previously been employed by his advertiser, his agency or other firms in the employ of the advertiser or his agency? If so, in what capacity?

6. What is the testifier's occupation(s)? If the testifier is a model or performer, how many print advertisements and how many broadcast commercials has the person participated in during the last two years?

7. If performance claims are made, what competency, in terms of experience and/or training, does the testifier have in evaluating the product or service (and, if applicable, competitive products or services) in the area in which he is testifying?

8. What instruction or guidance was given to the testifier prior to or during the production of the commercial?

9. Supply a witnessed or notarized affidavit signed by the testifier attesting to the truthfulness of his testimonial representation?

10. Supply a statement that, to the best of your knowledge, the testimonial is true.

AGENCY PRODUCER: _____

AGENCY: _____

DATE: _____

detail and stylistic subtleties. So-called magic moments do not happen by chance. These skillful bits of executional magic are built in through planning and the involvement of the director interacting with art director, writer and producer. This is the perfect opportunity for all creative participants to engage each other's best thinking and to achieve excellence prior to the shooting day. Inspiration rarely comes on set or can be accommodated without severe repercussions in time and money.

Casting is usually accomplished on tape. This may be a time saver, but it has its drawbacks. Certainly the people in charge of casting must know what they are looking for: that the model featured in a hair commercial has hair that displays manageability and shine or that the standup presenter can remember lines, read convincingly, serve as an embodiment of the target audience and possess overtones of the product character itself, for example.

The director should have as much input into the casting process and its outcome as possible since he or she has the responsibility for the final result and is undoubtedly the best judge of acting talent. In areas where the success of the advertising depends importantly on hair and skin, the performers should be called back just before final casting to make sure they have not been involved in another shooting where skin or hair has been damaged. (Print shootings are notorious for turning great hair into straw in a day.) Third call backs require additional payments and should be avoided if possible but are worth the price if necessary.

Wardrobe selection should be made at the pre-production meeting, not at the shooting. A stylist rushing about Manhattan while camera and crew sit idle is an unsettling experience for director, crew, talent and client—especially the last since the meter is ticking even when the camera is not turning.

By the end of the pre-production meeting, there must be no question in anyone's mind as to what is going to be happening on the set and what the final film will look like. Timetables for shooting and editing should be discussed once again. If any changes have been made that affect costs, these should be spelled out in dollar amounts by the agency and put down in writing for client signature. The agency should issue a call report of the meeting noting all agreements. This will undoubtedly be consistent with the pre-production agenda but may detail it further.

Sufficient time should be built in between pre-production and shooting—at least three days and preferably more—to allow the production company to ready itself without waste and permit the client to review the call report.

19

Managing a Cost-Effective Shooting

The best way for the you, the client, to manage the shooting day is not to go! Everything has been planned and decided. The agency and production company are all professionals. Allowing them to work independent of your scrutiny places responsibility clearly in their hands and drives them to accomplish your wishes. Your absence is both a compliment and a quiet reminder of your authority.

The best-managed shootings are largely mechanistic. Alfred Hitchcock observed toward the end of his career that he wished he could avoid the actual shooting itself; there was nothing left to do except record the action. Indeed, except for the newcomer to a set, most experienced hands describe the filmmaking process as something akin to watching paint dry. This is all to the good because filmmaking is a craft function, and all of those expensive craftsmen gathered together on the stage are paid by the hour.

Decision making on the set is always a last-minute change in plans, frequently the cause of substantial additional costs and often the origination of misguided efforts because of the pressure and overattention to minutiae that is so much a part of the shooting day. A well-planned shoot can begin to unravel quickly at the first break in continuity. Equally, the quality of the work suffers. Film has a peculiar sensitivity to the atmosphere in which it is exposed. The smell of confusion and tension somehow is absorbed by the material and is almost tangibly present later when the commercial is shown. Similarly, a commercial that is subjected to overstudy generates a sense of inertia regardless of the cutting pace artificially imposed on it later in the editorial process.

For all these reasons, it is best to work with what you have and let the professionals exercise their own talents free from distraction. If you have an advertising or production consultant on staff or on retainer, let that person attend the shooting in your stead.

Your major contribution in the production area is not your attendance at the shooting but rather your ability to come at the project with fresh eyes once the material has been shot and assembled. Even the agency staff have lost a good deal of objectivity because of their intimate association with the work. At that point, they may honestly not be able to see the forest for the trees, and your fresh viewpoint will be of considerable value.

If your presence is required on set for reasons of legal approval or assessment of tonality associated with the initiation of new advertising, there are some simple ways you can promote a positive atmosphere on the set and avoid costly overruns driven by indecision.

Keep the number of staff who come from the client side to a minimum. Only decision makers—those with the ability to contribute and the power to say yes or no with no question as to their authority— should attend. If brand assistants are invited to help further their education, closet them off to the side and make sure they understand that they are observers, not participants.

For every person who arrives from the client side, there is sure to be an agency counterpart. Sets are normally crowded places. The more people there are, the slower the shooting moves. At most successfully managed shootings, the account group and creatives show up briefly.

It is important to maintain a sense of discipline and decorum on the set. The director is in charge of what is happening in front of the camera; the producer is in charge of what is happening behind it. Any information or observations by the client should be relayed to the producer. If he or she finds the comments of value and importance, they will be relayed to the director at the appropriate moment.

One of the greatest contributors to a lack of discipline and cost overruns is the use of the on-set monitor. Typically, clusters of people from the client and agency sit around a fuzzy black-and-white image, mumbling and looking concerned. The director and crew watch the client and agency huddled about the monitor looking concerned.

Time, energy and focus are drained out of the proceedings and posited on the little box that is showing nothing much worth seeing.

The monitor does not give any semblance of what the motion picture camera is capturing in image, framing, lighting, color or vitality. To render an opinion of quality and workmanship based on what is being murkily transmitted to a 12-inch screen is something akin to asking an art critic to render a value judgment on a painting and supplying a poor photocopy on which to base this assessment.

Each fragment of film being shot does not encapsulate the entire commercial or have equal importance to the finished product. Film is a mosaic of bits and pieces assembled in editing. Few clients or agency members for that matter have the ability to put proper value against any piece as it contributes to the whole.

If framing, composition or lighting is of genuine concern to the client, viewing the scene through the camera lens is essential. Wait until lighting and direction and several takes have been accomplished, and then ask the producer for the opportunity to check the shot. This will take all of thirty seconds.

Pivotal here is your reliance on the director and the director of photography. Their eyes are the best judge of what the camera is getting. They are by nature perfectionists and will not want to move on until they are assured they have caught each setup as meticulously and artistically as possible. Both are already editing the film in their heads and assigning relative importance to each shot as it relates to the whole.

Repetitive takes—whether the result of the client, the agency or the production company—have gone well beyond any reasonable measure of perfection. By way of example, the ratio of shooting in filmed television programs is four to one: four takes exposed to achieve the one needed. Features work at a ratio of about ten to one. Commercials work at a ratio of forty to one and beyond. This mind-numbing practice is a classic example of works expanding to fill the time allotted. Nearly always, the third or fourth take is the final selection pulled in the screening room. Many talented directors even use the so-called camera rehearsal, when talent is most at ease.

If lighting is not changed, or the camera moved in or out or the director adjusting line readings or giving the talent additional bits of business, repetitive takes are just that. Your greatest contribution when this begins is to remind the company (and yourself) that this commercial is just one of a string of messages designed to get the news out about the product. It is not intended to take its place among the art treasures of Western civilization. Six months from now, you won't even be able to find a copy of the advertising or anyone who wants to look at it.

What about overtime and overages? The question here is, Who requests them, for what purpose and at what cost? Remember, you are in a firm bid situation. This means that the production company, director and agency have already agreed to a price and shooting schedule; you have a contract. If overtime is generated by the agency or the director, it is their responsibility to pick up all costs associated with overtime and overages. This is the purpose of the firm bid.

If you have requested some change that has caused the delay and inclusion of something new to the mix, that is another story. At this point, any change from the agreed specifications will trigger increases. It is essential that you give serious consideration to every change before you explore it with the agency or production company. You should always evaluate the variation on the basis of real need, not something "it would be nice to have in the can, just in case."

In authorizing any change or addition, be sure the agency producer receives an accurate cost forecast from the production company and determines whether this change is a number reflecting total cost: labor, materials, talent and so on. Production costs grow exponentially, one area triggering increases in other associated areas.

All overages should be recorded on a simple document reflecting who authorized the work to be done, its purpose, its costs and the date. These costs should be itemized in terms of gross cost to advertiser, even if some absolute specificity will not be available until later. The overage should be signed by the client originator—his or her name, not the name of the brand or company. The purpose of this is to make responsibility ongoing in terms of the brand group, division management and the agency itself.

A sample overage form is included for your examination (see Exhibit 19.1). Three copies of this overage form should be made: one for the agency producer, one for the account group and one for the client. This will be helpful later in helping all parties remember that the overage was authorized and who took responsibility for the additional cost.

Exhibit 19.1
Advertising Production Overage Approval Form

DIVISION: _____

PRODUCT: _____

COMMERCIAL / JOB TITLE: _____

ESTIMATE NUMBER: _____ OVERAGE APPROVAL NUMBER _____

AGENCY ORIGINATOR _____

*Description/Reason for Overage:

ESTIMATED COST: _____

ADVERTISING PRODUCTIONS APPROVAL: _____

DATE: _____

*If more than one item is involved, cost must be specified for each item and must total.

20

Editing Disciplines and Cost Control

There appears to be a surprising amount of confusion as to how the editing process is to be managed—and, indeed, the purpose of the editorial process itself. This accounts for editing costs' having risen from $8,000 per commercial just a few years ago to $40,000 and more being routinely spent in editing and post-production. Editing frequently represents as much as 20 percent of the entire production budget, spent in an after-the-fact manner. Editing is no longer accomplished in a week or so but often stretches over a period of months. This displacement of time triggers runaway costs, most of them largely unreported and accumulated only in an after-the-fact manner.

What is generating these enormous increases? Editors and other production professionals can give a number of reasons. Here are just a few.

Advent of tape as the editing medium. When commercials moved from film to film transferred to tape as the editing medium, per hour costs rose significantly. Tape editing is both more labor intensive and machine intensive than editing on film. The amount of technological change in tape equipment has been overwhelming. Machinery is becoming obsolete overnight. The expense of constantly retooling the machinery represents an enormous overhead expense, which is being passed on to the agency and client.

Availability of choice. Film editing was a laborious process. The film was actually cut and trimmed, with small pieces saved. A good deal of thought went into every cut before it was made. Because film was being intimately handled, there was a connection between those working on the material and the material itself. There was a respect for the material.

Tape has made editing faster and more impersonal. Although the work to be accomplished may be done in a fraction of the time, the overwhelming options tape has made available have actually slowed the process. Tape permits opportunities to store images and retrieve them; mix or manipulate images; add elements or remove them within the frame; change color, size or shapes; change image textures and speed of the action; and do mixes in the editing room of music, voice and sounds that before had to be done separately in another place. In short, the world's greatest train set has gotten more elaborate.

Number of people involved in the editing process. Editing has become a free-for-all, with more and more participants crowding into the editor's room. Reminiscent of the stateroom scene aboard ship in the Marx Brothers *A Night at the Opera,* editors tell of ten, twelve and more people squeezing themselves into the editorial suite, all of whom expect to edit the work simultaneously. Says an editor: "We once had a guy shouting out orders over the top of everyone else. We finally figured out this guy wasn't from the agency or the client. He was working on another job in the building, saw the crowd and just came in."

Lack of overall expertise. With the producer folded in to the creative group, editing has now become a democratic process. The art director, writer, account group, producer, creative director, brand manager, brand assistants, group supervisor, advertising manager, vice president of advertising and vice president of marketing all to view the material, comment and ask for alternate versions of the advertising. The only person who is not invited to participate is the director who shot the material and has a cutting pattern in mind. Who is the most professional participant supervising editing now? "It depends," says one editor. "I always go with the guy who doesn't hold the tape up to the light and ask, 'What happened to the pictures?' "

Many clients have lost their middle management ranks, especially those trained in film production and advertising management. Editing inside some companies is now regarded as a reward for the brand manager—a chance for this person to "play producer." Eventually the final decision will be made by upper-division management doing their own series of cuts. The editing process has thus become both a playground and a parade ground inside client headquarters and inside agencies to see who has the rank and clout to decide the final cut.

Development of the non-linear commercial. With the rise of the image commercial, sometimes known as the life-style and art director commercial, commercials are now comprised of unconnected, independent scenes that may be arranged in any order. Since the advertising message is relayed through an announcer track, commercials are not dialogue driven. This permits the possibility of endless reshuffling of elements. Thus, not only is image advertising more expensive to shoot, it is susceptible to change and difficult to control after shooting because editing is not so much subject to objective scrutiny on the part of the client as it is a subjective decision on the part of the agency creative team. The commercial is never finished in this sense; the agency merely decides to stop working on it. When? In the words of the current advertising slogan, "It just feels right."

The editorial process thus reveals a great deal about client and agency motives, their thoughts about advertising and the advertising process, their level of expertise in the advertising area and the level of permissible waste allowed to "keep the creative group happy" and "let the brand manager play producer."

Returning the editorial process to a professional footing and managing its costs is a fairly simple matter for the client who elects to do this. Editing should be done in accordance with the storyboard and the pre-production agenda as approved by the client. The director, producer and editor should be the only participants in the editing suite. The director should supervise the cut as a continuation of the filmic process and along the lines he or she had in mind in shooting the commercial.

The agency should formally review the edited version in one meeting, not in successive meetings generating successive versions. No extensive revisions, mixes or post-production finishing should be attempted until the client has had an opportunity to see the material.

A firm cost ceiling of $8,000 should be set on the assemblage of the footage for the first client screening. This screening should be understood to represent work in progress. At this meeting, all elements of the client management team should be present. The client's representative in the production process, hopefully some production agent, will be responsible for articulating the next steps in terms accessible to the agency producer in obvious concurrence with the wishes of brand and division management.

The agency producer should put an approximate value on the cost of this work before next steps occur. This again provides the client with a value equation as to whether any suggested changes are worth the cost of implementing them.

Whoever authorizes the overage should sign a separate overage form for every change requested. Special opticals should be paid as a legitimate overage. All other overages generated in the editorial process should be reviewed in terms of cost and progress achieved at each step. At the completion of the advertising, all versions of the commercial should be screened in consecutive order to establish the necessity and the improvement brought about by these changes. Each client manager should find his or her performance rating and compensation affected by his or her decisions in this area as well as in the original selection of advertising to be approved and its costs.

Indeed, brand managers who are asked or who wish to participate in film production should be persuaded to attend outside film courses as part of their orientation process and serve a period of apprenticeship at a film company or editorial house. This will bring their skill levels up to only about the level of a studio production trainee, but at least they will gain some sense of the overall process and some semblance of understanding the craftsmanship that goes into filmmaking and its cost implications.

The agency should be expected to absorb all editorial and post-production costs not authorized by the client or approved by means of the overage approval form. Agency competence should be judged on how quickly and competently advertising is completed for client viewing.

There should be no "creative fee" paid to the editorial house. The proper exercise of the editor's responsibility is to work creatively. In a similar manner, the copywriter is not expected to be told to work creatively or to expect to be paid extra for doing so.

Many clients are turning over post-production work after editing to completion services, which eliminate editing house markup on what are essentially mechanical steps. You may well want to consider the savings in such consolidation among all agencies along with consolidation of all tape dupes of finished advertising with a single supplier. Significant savings may be realized by consolidation in both areas.

21

Final Costs: Actual Versus Estimated

Every producer has a job jacket—a manila folder that holds all information associated with the television commercial. This is usually handed off to the business affairs department at the agency, which matches invoices, collates the information and sends it off to the account group, which reviews it and then forwards it to you, the client, for inspection, review and payment.

Jobs should be closed out in ninety days or less. Truly buttoned-up agencies accomplish this in forty-five days. The sooner they do, the better. Details associated with any particular shoot become harder and harder to reconstruct and remember with the passage of time.

The final actual costs of your commercial should be easily assessed. The original dollar figure reflected in the firm bid estimate should be adjusted up only on the basis of authorized increases as reflected on the overage form.

Final actual costs should be reflected on the cost estimate, by category of expense. If there is any discrepancy, the agency should be questioned as to why the discrepancy exists. With no apologies, the agency should be expected to absorb all cost overruns not triggered by client request. Equally, bills not collected within specific time frames—the ninety-day closeout or the end of the fiscal year—should be returned to the agency for payment by them.

One client persuaded by his agency that this placed too much pressure on the agency found himself paying bills "suddenly discovered in somebody's bottom drawer" two years after work was completed. This made a hash of current spending plans.

Final actual costs should be displayed next to estimated costs on the same form and reviewed for accuracy by your production representative. This person or the senior division manager assigned this responsibility should authorize final payment. A sample broadcast production estimate for this purpose is furnished here for your inspection (see Exhibit 21.1).

Exhibit 21.1
Broadcast Production Estimate

DATE:

AGENCY: JOB NO: ESTIMATE NO: AGENCY PRODUCER: BUSINESS MANAGER: ACCOUNT EXECUTIVE:	CLIENT: PRODUCT: TELEVISION: Full Finished ( ) Test ( ) RADIO: ( ) ORIGINAL ( ) REVISED ( ) FINAL ACTUAL ( )

ISCI CODE NO.	COMMERCIAL TITLE/DESCRIPTION	LENGTH
1.		
2.		
3.		
4.		
5.		
6.		

PRODUCTION COMPANIES BID	AMOUNT	TALENT BREAKDOWN		
1.	$	# On-Camera Principals:	# Days/Hrs:	
2.	$	# Off-Camera Principals:	# Days/Hrs:	
3.	$	# Handmodels:	# Days/Hrs:	
4.	$	# General Extras:	# Days/Hrs:	

SUMMARY - RECOMMENDED PRODUCTION BID

Pre-Pro Days: # Prelight Days:
Build/Strike Days: Hrs:
Studio Shoot Days: Hrs:
Location Days: Hrs:
Location Site:
1. Pre-Pro & Wrap Costs $
2. Shooting Crew Labor $
3. Location & Travel Exp. $
4. Props,Wardrobe,Animals $
5. Studio & Set Construct. $
6. Equipment Costs $
7. Film, Develop & Print $
8. Miscellaneous $
9.   SUB-TOTAL: A to K $_____
10.Director/Creative Fees $
11.Insurance (%) $
12.Production Fee (%) $
13.Talent Costs & Expenses $
14.Editorial & Finishing $
15.   PRODUCTION BID TOTAL $_____

COMMENTS:

SUMMARY - ENTIRE BROADCAST PRODUCTION ESTIMATE

	ORIGINAL	REV/FINAL
A. Production Bid Total	$	$
B. Animation	$	$
C. Editorial	$	$
D. Videotape Completion	$	$
E. Original Music	$	$
F. Stock Music	$	$
G. Studio Record/Mix	$	$
H. Sound Effects	$	$
I. Casting	$	$
J. Talent Session Fees/P&W	$	$
K. Talent Travel Expenses	$	$
L. Artwork/Titles	$	$
M. Product/Package Prep	$	$
N. Other:_____	$	$
O. Other:_____	$	$
P. Other:_____	$	$
Q. Other:_____	$	$
R. TOTAL NET PROD COST	$_____	$_____
S. Agency Comssn. (%)	$	$
T. Payroll Taxes/Handling	$	$
U. Sales Taxes	$	$
V. Shipping/Messengers	$	$
W. Cassettes	$	$
X. Storyboards/Photostats	$	$
Y. Agency Travel Expenses	$	$
Z. Other:	$	$
Aa.Other:_____	$	$
Bb.Other:_____	$	$
Cc.Other:_____	$	$
Dd. TOTAL GROSS PROD COST	$_____	$_____

APPROVAL SIGNATURES
Agency Representative:_____

Client Representative:_____

22

Creative, Production and Cost Controls in Print

The cost of print for national advertisers has risen at about an equivalent rate to what has been happening in television—about 250 percent in the past ten years.

The disciplines that may be applied to television production may also be applied to print. Indeed, such disciplines must be applied because print, if anything, is more exacting in terms of creativity than that associated with television. Print does not offer the wide range of contributory elements—motion, sound, music, quick cuts and post-production devices—that may be called into service in television to shore up a weak selling idea. Yet print faces just as much competition as television. The comparison of advertising pages to editorial content in any magazine will give you a quick idea of print clutter.

Print demands greater participation by the reader than does television, where the passive viewer may simply have the set on. The reader has much more control than the television viewer in attending to advertising or dismissing it. He or she can slow down the attention process or speed it up with a quick glance or by turning the page. Print demands greater focus, greater persuasion and a true headline idea and visual that clearly encapsulates the advertiser's message.

Creatively, print may reiterate what the advertiser is saying in television (and should) but also penetrate the consumer's awareness at a deeper level through the inclusion of much greater depth, detail and factual support. This permits greater expansion and exposition of the reason that one product is superior in some characteristic, product performance area or overall capability.

Print also reinforces product name and package registration and can offer specific or supportive benefits, such as recipes for food products, maintenance and application (how to get better mileage from your car) or how to protect your home (with a specific paint or stain).

The ground rules for reviewing print copy are the same as reviewing creative choices in television:

1. Is the advertising on strategy?
2. Is my product the hero of the advertising?
3. Is the selling idea single-minded?
4. Is the product benefit visualized?
5. Is there a clear end benefit for the user?
6. Is the target audience featured?
7. Is the setting natural, reflecting where and how the product is actually used?
8. Does the selling idea set my brand apart from the competition?
9. Does the ad generate an immediate impulse to buy?

Print and its costs and development timetable should be planned in advance at the time the spending plan is being developed: how many ads, needed when, as a continuation of what has come before or redesigned to reflect some new marketing effort, a package change, a product improvement, a flanker brand. Again, specific cost ceilings and timetables should grow out of the calendar of events that is provided by the spending plan.

Copy and layout development usually demand the same time frame as television copy—eight weeks. Approximately another thirteen weeks are needed for looking at examples of the photographer's work, defining specs, checking availabilities, casting, bidding, negotiating, pre-production, shooting, retouching, offset separations and the like.

Again, a first-need basis should be determined as the due date for print production. A print production timetable is provided for your examination, as is a print production project initiation form (see Exhibits 22.1 and 22.2)).

Special casting requirements should be provided in writing by the client to the account group. If casting presents any unique challenges, the schedule may have to be expanded. Be on the lookout for new

Exhibit 22.1
Print Production Timetable

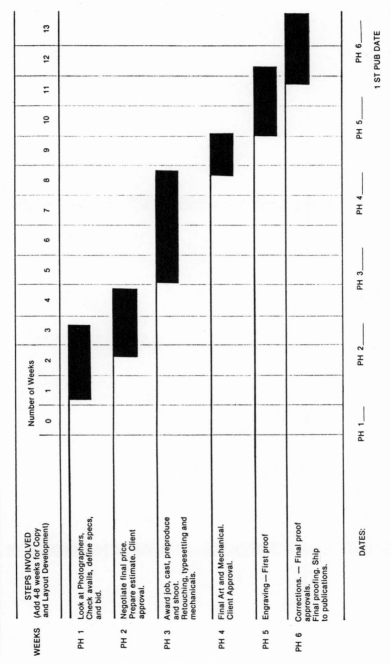

Exhibit 22.2
Print Production Project Initiation

DIVISION _____   DATE _____

BRAND _____   ESTIMATE NO. _____

AGENCY _____   AGENCY JOB NO. _____

PRINT: SIZE _____ # OF COLORS _____   AGENCY ORIGINATOR _____

DESCRIPTION

_____

_____

_____

_____

WEEKS TO 1st CLOSING**		ORIGINAL DATE	REVISED DATE
17	PROJECT INITIATION _____	_____	_____
13	FIRST COPY/LAYOUT PRESENTATION (4)* _____	_____	_____
11	SECOND COPY/LAYOUT PRESENTATION (2)* _____	_____	_____
10	THIRD COPY/LAYOUT PRESENTATION (1)* _____	_____	_____
8	LAYOUT/COPY APPD. _____	_____	_____
8	LEGAL APPL. _____	_____	_____
8	SUBMIT OVERSCALE CONTRACTS FOR REVIEW _____	_____	_____
8	ESTIMATE APPROVED (2)* _____	_____	_____
4	ART & MECHANICAL COMPL. (4)* _____	_____	_____
2.5	ENGRAVING 1st PROOF (1.5)* _____	_____	_____
1	FINAL PROOF (1.5)* _____	_____	_____
0	SHIP TO PUBLICATIONS (1)* _____	_____	_____

*(Minimum number of weeks)

REMARKS

** CLOSING DATES USUALLY 15th OF 3rd MONTH PRECEDING DATE OF ISSUE talent, who also may be of benefit to you in your television advertising. Some advertisers couple television and print shootings to generate economies in sets and costumes and to accommodate tight time frames. Your agency will be able to decide if this represents a genuine opportunity for you.

Head sheets and day rates for proposed models should be reviewed by you, the client. Overscale talent, and many print models essentially generate overscale rates, requires careful examination of specific terms and usage provisions. The talent buy sheet already provided for overscale talent and the overscale talent contract should be used by the agency. While exclusivity is desirable, print models are notorious for appearing in competitors' ads. Any genuine exclusivity will require substantial sums—often over $1 million—to make a famous face truly yours.

In print as in television, avoid the practice of flying photographers and talent from one coast to another. Eliminate paying for an entourage, especially in the use of star talent and their demands for special makeup and hair stylists. By no means grant even star talent the right to dictate creative intent or terms or usage, where print may appear, what size and other parameters. Agents' fees are to be deducted from what is paid to the talent, not placed atop fees as an additional expense.

As in television, you should establish buying policies and maintain a realistic posture in the face of creative demands:

1. Eliminate the need for the pre-light day.
2. Eliminate multiple shooting days.
3. Eliminate large sets and stages.
4. Eliminate overpriced and unnecessary equipment.
5. Eliminate alternate shots.
6. Eliminate location shootings if possible.
7. Eliminate actual night shootings.
8. Eliminate single bids.
9. Eliminate color-correcting product unnecessarily.

In discussing creative elements, remember the value of close-ups, and eliminate all elements that do not directly feed into the product sale, product performance and product differentiation. The simpler the composition is and the closer the subject is to the camera, the fewer surround elements will be needed and needed to be bought.

Waste in print is generated exactly as it is in television: overbuying time, manpower and materials because decision making was not thorough and creative intent not articulated in advance.

Remember how much definition will be lost when size is reduced—for example, in *TV Guide*. Remember too, elements that may be stripped in. You do not need to go to the Eiffel Tower to have it appear in the ad background.

Never include bright, hot background colors, particularly when shooting skin, hair or food. These colors will spill forward as much as 6 feet and contaminate objects in front of them. (This is true for television as well as print.) White backgrounds should be used at the original shooting with hot background colors stripped in later.

Insist on complete and detailed specifications for the bidding of print in writing. If you have an advertising or production expert on staff or retainer, this person should review and agree to all specifications before bidding begins.

All print production should be competitively bid with at least three suppliers in photography, illustration and production. Looking for resources outside the major production areas of New York and Los Angeles can significantly reduce costs of creative and production elements. Whenever possible, reuse previously shot materials and examine the cost economies generated by pooling print jobs.

So as not to extend the bidding process unnecessarily, you may want to exempt any elements costing below $2,500 from competitive bidding. This is entirely up to you, as is the dollar limit for exception.

All elements of the shooting—equipment, film, props, costumes—should be broken out individually so that comparability may be examined on a category-by-category basis from bid to bid. As with television production, since specifications are identical, costs may be examined on a line-by-line basis. Even the low bidder may be higher in one category, and this element may be isolated for negotiation.

Work should represent a "buyout," and no additional "creative or use fees" should be necessary or allowed. Many photographers have begun asking for separate payments for each use of the material—that is, additional payments for brochures or point of purchase. Whenever possible, ask the agency to bid photographers who do not attempt to build in restrictive clauses. As in television production, there are hundreds of talented people who are eager to work under conditions more advantageous to the client. There is never only one photographer who is right for the job.

Exhibit 22.3
Sample Print Production Estimate Form

ART PREPARATION:	Original	Revised	PRODUCTION:	Original	Revised
Layout-Comp			Typography		
Illustration			Electronic		
Stock Photo/Illus.			Retouching		
			Offset		
Photography Fee			Separations		
Photo Travel Expenses			Progressive		
Equipment Rental			Proofs		
Location Scouting			Production		
Location Fees			Overtime		
Casting			Duplicate Matls.		
Model Fees			Printing		
Model Expenses			Reprints		
Stylist			Other		
Photo Assistants					
Make-Up/Hair					
Home Economist					
Props/Wardrobe					
Film/Processing					
Background/Surfaces					
Insurance					
Messengers					
Dye Transfers					
Retouching					
"C" Prints					
Chromes/					
Transparencies					
B&W Conversions					
Mechanicals					
Photostats			TOTAL PRODUCTION		
			RECAP ART PREP		
			Agency Comssion		
			Sales Tax		
			Agency Travel		
TOTAL ART PREPARATION			GROSS TOTAL		

COMMENTS:

Carefully examine the internals of all bids to eliminate such items as production assistants, meals and miscellaneous charges. As with television, props and costumes should be rented whenever possible rather than purchased. If purchase is necessary, these items should be considered the property of the client and disposed of at his or her instructions. (General provisions and instructions for the disposal of props should be part of an advertising procedures manual for television as well as print.) Many advertisers donate the items to charity and retain the receipts for tax purposes.

Exhibit 22.4
Print Production Overage Approval Form

DIVISION: _____

PRODUCT: _____

COMMERCIAL / JOB TITLE: _____

ESTIMATE NUMBER: _____ OVERAGE APPROVAL NUMBER _____

AGENCY ORIGINATOR _____

*Description/Reason for Overage:

ESTIMATED COST: _____

ADVERTISING PRODUCTION APPROVAL: _____

DATE: _____

*If more than one item is involved, cost must be specified for each item and must total.

A pre-production meeting should be held for print exactly as it is for television. All creative aspects of the production should be discussed, and the meeting should not end until agreement is reached by all parties as to intent and time frames. The agency producer may or may not be required to participate in the print shooting. If costs have been escalating rapidly on your business, by all means make this person's participation mandatory and responsibility central.

Cost contingencies in print, as in television, should not be allowed. As is also true in television, post-production costs should not be built into the bid in advance until the work has been seen by the client.

Invoices from all suppliers in shooting, retouching, illustration, typography and mechanical should be examined by the agency and sent forward for client approval along with final costs.

All overages generated by the agency without client approval should be absorbed by the agency. Overages generated by the client should be detailed on an overage form that identifies costs, reason for change or purpose, the date and the individual who authorized the work.

A sample print production estimate form and a print production overage approval form are supplied here for your examination (see Exhibits 22.3 and 22.4).

23

Some Final Thoughts

My aim in this book has not been to make you a copywriter or producer or even anything approaching a cost expert in the business of approving and managing advertising. What I have tried to do is to demystify the process to some degree and to impress on you that the buying of advertising is little different from the buying of any other goods or services.

The client-agency partnership so often described by agency management as the optimal relationship is probably an unrealistic and unattainable goal. It may not even be in the best interests of either party. Clearly no genuine partnership can exist unless both parties are able to share in the profitability of the other and both are prepared to make good on any losses originating from incompetence, shoddy workmanship or the poor management of time and dollars. I do not anticipate marketers' slicing off a portion of their proceeds to agencies when a brand goes through the roof, nor can I imagine any agency's cheerfully refunding the client's money when its advertising fails to recall successfully or generate substantial public interest in the marketplace.

Rather than a partnership, there is something like a symbiotic relationship between advertiser and agency. The agency depends on the client to develop a product worth shouting about; the advertiser depends on the agency to know something about selling and how to fashion a commercial or print ad that arrests viewers, interests and excites their imagination and builds in a genuine desire to examine a product and buy it.

Clearly, it is not the agencies' business to attempt to build in worth or value by smoke and mirrors. The public is far too smart to buy any product more than once because of its image. Successful advertising probably shortens life expectancy for an inferior brand because more people will find out faster if the product does not live up to its billing.

A level of comparability thus must be expected about product worth, advertiser expectation and agency competence. Comparability is possible only when both the client and the agency meet on a certain level of expertise and with a well-enunciated standard of expectation.

Advertising success and advertising costs are essentially a matching of expectation and performance. Both are outgrowths of agency and company management competence. The agency in many ways is only as good as the client. Certainly clients always gets what they ask for, whether they like it or not.

Appendixes

Appendix A
AICP Videotape Production Cost Summary

	Bid Date	Actualization Date	
Production Co.:	Agency:	Agency job #	
Address:	Client:	Product:	
Telephone No.:	Job #		
Production Contact:	Agency prod:	Tel:	
Director:	Agency art dir:	Tel:	
Director of Photography:	Agency writer:	Tel:	
Set Designer:	Agency Bus. Mgr.:	Tel:	
Editor:	Commercial title:	No.:	Length:
No. pre-prod. days	pre-light/rehearse	1.	
No. build/strike days	Hours:	2.	
No. Studio shoot days	Hours:	3.	
No. Location days	Hours:	4.	
Location sites:		5.	
		6.	

SUMMARY OF ESTIMATED PRODUCTION COSTS		ESTIMATED	ACTUAL		
21. Pre-production and wrap costs	Totals A & C				
22. Shooting crew labor	Total B				
23. Location and travel expenses	Total D				
24. Props, wardrobe, animals	Total E				
25. Studio & Set Construction Costs	Totals F, G, and H				
26. Equipment costs	Total I				
27. Videotape Stock	Total J				
28. Miscellaneous	Total K				
29.	Sub-Total: A to K				
30. Director/creative fees (Not Included In Direct Cost)	Total L				
31. Insurance					
32.	Sub-Total: Direct Costs				
33. Production Fee					
34. Talent costs and expenses	Totals M and N				
35. Editorial and finishing per:					
36.					
37.	Grand Total (Including Director's Fee)				
38. Contingency					

Comments:

Appendix A (continued)

CREW	A: PRE-PRO/WRAP ESTIMATED				A: PRE-PRO/WRAP ACTUAL					B: SHOOT ESTIMATED				B: SHOOT ACTUAL			
	Days	Rate	O/T Hrs	Total	Days	Rate	O/T $	Total		Days	Rate	O/T Hrs	Total	Days	Rate	O/T $	Total
301 Producer:									351								
302 Assistant Director:									352								
303 Associate Director:									353								
304 Stage Manager:									354								
305 Director Photography:									355								
306 Lighting Director:									356								
307 Camera Operator:									357								
308									358								
309									359								
310 Camera Asst:									360								
311 VTR Operator:									361								
312									362								
313 Video Engineer:									363								
314 Outside Prop:									364								
315 Inside Prop:									365								
316									366								
317									367								
318 Electrician:									368								
319									369								
320									370								
321 Grip:									371								
322									372								
323									373								
324 Sound Mixer :									374								
325 Sound Boom:									375								
326 Sound Recordist:									376								
327 Sound Playback:									377								
328 Make-Up:									378								
329 Hair:									379								
330 Stylist:									380								
331 Wardrobe Attendant:									381								
332 Script Supervisor:									382								
333 Home Economist:									383								
334 Asst. Home Economist:									384								
335 Special Efx:									385								
336 Scenic:									386								
337 Telepr. Operator:									387								
338 Generator Operator:									388								
339 Still Photographer:									389								
340 Loc. Contact/Scout:									390								
341 P.A.									391								
342 2nd A.D.									392								
343 Nurse:									393								
344 Craft Service:									394								
345 Fire Fighter:									395								
346 Police Officer:									396								
347 Wtfr./Techr.:									397								
348 Teamster									398								
349									399								
350									400								
	Sub Total A									Sub Total B							
	PT/P & W									PT/P & W							
	TOTAL A									TOTAL B							

Appendix A (continued)

PRE-PRODUCTION & WRAP/MATERIALS & EXPENSES	ESTIMATED	ACTUAL	
351 Auto Rentals (No. of Cars)			
352 Air Fares: No. of people ( ) x Amount per fare ( )			
353 Per Diems: No. of people ( ) x Amount per day ( )			
354 Still Camera Rental & Film -			
355 Messengers			
356 Trucking			
357 Deliveries & Taxis			
358 Home Economist Supplies			
359 Telephone & Cable			
360 Casting Call/Prep____ Days Casting____Days Call Back ____Days			
361 . Casting Facilities			
362. Working Meals			
363.			
Sub Total C			

LOCATION EXPENSES	ESTIMATED	ACTUAL	
364. Location Fees			
365. Permits			
366. Car Rentals			
367. Bus Rentals			
368. Camper Dressing Room Vehicles			
369. Parking, Tolls, & Gas			
370. Trucking			
371. Other vehicles			
372. Other vehicles			
373. Customs			
374. Air freight/ Excess baggage			
375. Air Fares: No. of people ( ) x cost per fare ( )			
376. Per Diems: Total No. man days ( ) x amt. per day ( )			
377. Air fares: No. of people ( ) x cost per fare ( )			
378. Per Diems: Total No. man days ( ) x amt. per day ( )			
379. Breakfast: No. of man days ( ) x amt. per person ( )			
380. Lunch: No. of man days ( ) x amt. per person ( )			
381. Dinner: No. of man days ( ) x amt. per person ( )			
382. Guards			
383. Limousines (Celebrity Service)			
384. Cabs and Other Transportation			
385. Kit Rental			
386. Art Work			
387. Gratuities			
388.			
389.			
Sub Total D			

PROPS AND WARDROBE & ANIMALS	ESTIMATED	ACTUAL	
390. Prop Rental			
391. Prop Purchase			
392. Wardrobe Rental			
393. Wardrobe Purchase			
394. Picture Vehicles			
395. Animals & Handlers			
396. Wigs & Mustaches			
397. Color Correction			
398.			
399.			
400.			
Sub Total E			

Appendix A (continued)

STUDIO RENTAL & EXPENSES—STAGE	ESTIMATED				ACTUAL			
	Days	Hrs	Rate	Total	Days	Hrs	Rate	Total
401. Rental for Build Days								
402. Rental for Build O.T. Hours								
403. Rental for Pre-Lite Days								
404. Rental for Pre-Lite O.T. Hours								
405. Rental for Shoot Days								
406. Rental for Shoot O.T. Hours								
407. Rental for Strike Days								
408. Rental for Strike O.T. Hours								
409. Generator & Operator								
410. Set Guards								
411. Total Power Charge & Bulbs								
412. Misc. Studio Charges (Cartage, Phone, Coffee)								
413. Meals for Crew & Talent (Lunch, Dinner)								
414.								
415.								
416.								
417.								
Sub Total F								

SET CONSTRUCTION (CREW FOR BUILD, STRIKE, PRELIGHT)	ESTIMATED				ACTUAL			
	Days	Rate	O/T Hrs.	Total	Days	Rate	O/T $	Total
418. Set Designer Name:								
419. Carpenters								
420. Grips								
421. Outside Props								
422. Inside Props								
423. Scenics								
424. Electricians								
425. Teamsters								
426. Crew for Strike								
427. P.A.s								
428.								
429.								
430.								
		Sub Total G						
		PT/P & W						
		TOTAL G						

SET CONSTRUCTION MATERIALS	ESTIMATED	ACTUAL	
431. Props (Set Dressing Purchase)			
432. Props (Set Dressing Rental)			
433. Lumber			
434. Paint			
435. Hardware			
436. Special Effects			
437. Special Outside Construction			
438. Trucking			
439. Messengers/Deliveries			
440. Kit Rental			
441.			
442.			
Sub Total H			

Appendix A (continued)

EQUIPMENT RENTAL	ESTIMATED	ACTUAL	
443. Videotape Camera Rental (Number)			
Special Lenses			
Videotape Recorder Rental (Number Format)			
Videotape Recorder Rental (Number Format)			
Stage Pkg./Videotape Equip. (Days/Hours)			
VTR (Number Format)			
VTR (Number Format)			
Number of cameras			
Studio Included Yes ____ No ____			
Location pkg. Mobile Van (Days/Hours)			
VTR's number Format			
VTR's number Format			
Number of cameras			
444. Sound Rental			
445. Lighting Rental			
446. Grip Rental			
447. Generator Rental			
448. Crane/Cherry Picker Rental			
449. Additional Monitors			
450. Special Effects/Graphic Equip (Specify)			
451. Walkie Talkies, Bull Horns			
452. Dolly Rental			
453. Camera Car			
454. Helicopter			
455. Production Supplies			
456. Teleprompter			
457.			
458.			
Sub Total I			

VIDEOTAPE STOCK	ESTIMATED			ACTUAL		
	Min./Hr.	Cost Pr. Min./Hr.	TOTAL	Min./Hr.	Cost Pr. Min./Hr.	TOTAL
459. Purchase Tape Stock (Hours/Minutes) Format)						
460. Purchase Tape Stock (Hours/Minutes) Format)						
461. Rental Tape Stock (Hours/Minutes) Format)						
462. Rental Tape Stock (Hours/Minutes) Format)						
463. Sound Transfer						
464. Screen Dailies						
465.						
466.						
Sub Total J						

MISCELLANEOUS COSTS	ESTIMATED	ACTUAL	
467. Petty Cash			
468. Air Shipping/Special Carriers			
469. Phones and Cables			
470. Accountable Cash Expenditures Under $15 Each			
471. External Billing Costs (Computer Accounting, etc.)			
472. Special Insurance			
473.			
474.			
Sub Total K			

DIRECTOR/CREATIVE FEES	ESTIMATED	ACTUAL	
475. Prep			
476. Travel			
477. Shoot Days			
478. Post-production			
479.			
480.			
481.			
Sub Total L			

Appendix A (continued)

TALENT	No.	Rate	Days	TRAVEL DAYS	O/T Hrs 1½x	2x	ESTIMATED	No.	Days	ACTUAL
234. O/C Principals										
235. O/C Principals										
236. O/C Principals										
237. O/C Principals										
238. O/C Principals										
239. O/C Principals										
240. O/C Principals										
241. O/C Principals										
242. O/C Principals										
243. O/C Principals										
244.										
245.										
246.										
247. General Extras										
248. General Extras										
249. General Extras										
250. General Extras										
251. General Extras										
252. General Extras										
253.										
254.										
255.										
256. Hand Model										
257.										
258.										
259. Voice Over										
260. Fitting Fees: S.A.G./AFTRA										
261. Fitting Fees: S.E.G.										
262.										
263. Audition Fees: S.A.G./AFTRA										
264. Audition Fees: S.E.G.										
265.										
Sub Total										
266. Payroll & P&W Taxes										
267. Wardrobe Allowance: No. of talent ( ) x No. of garments ( ) x fee per garment ( ).										
268.										
Sub Total										
269. Other										
270. Mark-up										
Sub Total M										

TALENT EXPENSES	ESTIMATED	ACTUAL	
271. Per diem: No. of man days ( ) x amount per day ( )			
272. Air fare: No. of people ( ) x amount per fare ( )			
273. Cabs and other transportation			
274. Mark-Up			
275.			
276.			
Sub Total N			

Appendix A (continued)

Editorial Company or Production Company		Bid Date		Actualization Date	
		Agency:		Agency Job #	
Address:		Client:		Product:	
Telephone No.:					
Post Production Contact:		Agency prod:		Tel:	
Editor		Agency art dir:		Tel:	
Director		Agency writer:		Tel:	
		Agency Bus. Mgr.:		Tel:	
		Commercial title:		No.:	Length:
		1.			
		2.			
		3.			
		4.			
		5.			
		6.			

SUMMARY OF ESTIMATED VIDEOTAPE POST PRODUCTION COSTS			ESTIMATED	ACTUAL
40	Editorial Fixed Package Price (where applicable)	Total P		
41	Videotape Editorial	Total Q		
42	Film/Tape, Tape/Film Transfers	Total R		
43	Sound, Recording Music, Mix	Total S		
44	Completion Materials	Total T		
45	Other	Total U		
46	Director/Editor Creative Supervision Fee	Total V		
47	Sub-Total: Direct Costs			
48	Mark-up			
49	Grand Total			
50				
51				

Comments:

Appendix A (continued)

SUMMARY OF ESTIMATED VIDEOTAPE POST PRODUCTION COSTS	ESTIMATED	ACTUAL
501 Fixed Package Price (where applicable)		
Sub Total P		

502 Videotape Editorial		
503 Editing on-line No. VTR or other editing equip. hours of editing Format/Technology		
504 Editing off-line No. VTR or other editing equip. hours of editing Format/Technology		
505 Conforming off-line to on-line, hours format (to) format		
506 Videotape transfer, format (to) format		
rental stock _____ (or) purchase stock _____		
507 coding		
508 art work (titles etc.)		
509 camera hours		
510 video generate titles, pre-program hours in use hours		
511 special effects equipment, hours format/technology		
512 special effects equipment, hours format/technology		
513 tape stock for editing, minutes rental _____ (or) purchase _____		
514		
515		
Sub Total Category Q		

517 Film/Tape, Tape/Film Transfers		
518 tape to film transfer, negative mm screen minutes technology,		
includes negative _____ (or) doesn't include negative _____		
519 separate cost of film negative if not included in 518		
520 film prints from film negative, number/mm number/mm		
521 film to tape transfer, hours supervised (or) hours unsupervised		
silent interlock composite		
from 16mm (or) from 35mm		
to what videotape format includes tape stock _____ (or) doesn't include stock _____		
522		
523		
Sub Total Category R		

525 Sound Recordings, Music and Mix		
526 stock music		
527 original music		
528 sound effects		
529 sound transfer, hours		
530 dubbing studio, hours		
531 studio for narration, hours		
with film projection _____ (or) with tape playback _____ (or) without picture playback _____		
532 studio for sound mixing, hours with tape playback _____		
(or) with film projection _____ (or) without picture playback _____		

Appendix A (continued)

SUMMARY OF ESTIMATED VIDEOTAPE POST PRODUCTION COSTS		ESTIMATED	ACTUAL
533	audio retrack to videotape, (to) format		
534			
535			
	Sub Total Category S		

537	Completion Materials		
538	videotape master, quantity format		
539	printing duplicate tape, quantity format		
540	printing duplicate tape, quantity format		
541	videotape dubs, quantity format		
542	videotape dubs, quantity format		
543	videotape dubs, quantity format		
544	video cassettes, quantity format		
545	video cassettes, quantity format		
546	supplies, boxes, reels, cans		
547	video disc master, quantity format		
548	video disc copies, quantity format		
549	video disc copies, quantity format		
550			
551			
	Sub Total Category T		

553	Other		
554	standards conversion (i.e. NTSC to PAL), hours standard (to) standard		
	the "to" stock rented _____ (or) stock purchased _____		
555	standards conversion (i.e. NTSC to PAL), hours standard (to) standard		
	the "to" stock rented _____ (or) stock purchased _____		
556	videotape screenings, hours format		
557	shipping/freight/messenger		
558	customs		
559	storage facilities, storage months state		
560	phones/cables		
561	external billings costs (computer accounting)		
562	petty cash		
563	insurance		
564			
565			
	Sub Total Category U		

567	Director and/or Editor Creative Supervision Fee		
568			
569			
	Sub Total Category V		

160

Appendix B
AICP Glossary

The basis of the "Glossary" obviously was the A.I.C.P. form. When preparing this lexicon, it became evident that, because we have to deal with many different unions and customs in various parts of the U.S., we do not all use the same words to describe job functions and other costs. Rather than attempt to qualify each term for local custom and usage, a specific frame of reference was used that may not be particularized to your individual need.

CATEGORY A/B

1/51 Producer: The liaison throughout the job, between the agency/client and the director/crew. He/she helps create a positive atmosphere for the production. The producer is the channel of communication who helps to interpret the needs of the agency into specific goals that can be achieved by the production company. The producer retains overall responsibility for the budget and identifies overage areas as they occur.

In preparation, the producer attends talent callbacks, is present on location scouts, attends production meetings and, in general, supervises the preparation of the job. On the set, the producer is available to the agency/client to facilitate communications with the director.

2/52 Assistant Director: The "right arm" of the director, both in organizing the production, and in running the set. In preparation the A.D. surveys the location, analyzes the job, and coordinates various logistic elements of the production. The A.D. suggests a shooting schedule, sets the call times, and coordinates with the crew department heads to determine personnel requirements; in general, the A.D. works with the producer and director to set up the job in the most efficient manner possible. On the shoot the A.D. runs the set, working closely with the director to anticipate his needs and communicate them to the crew. In addition, the A.D. is responsible for directing any background action, and maintaining order on the set.

3/53 Director of Photography: Responsible for the overall visual 'look' of the film. The D.P. surveys the location and/or sets, and then interprets all this information into technical terms, deciding what equipment and manpower will be needed to achieve the desired results. The D.P. will communicate his needs to the production staff, and advise the A.D. as to the time he will need to set up each shot, so the A.D. can plan the shooting in an efficient way. On the shoot, the D.P. supervises the camera and lighting crew and, in many cases, physically operates the camera. Note: In the commercial field, many directors are also D.P.'s and also camera operators, i.e. they light and operate, as well as direct.

4/54 Camera Operator: In those instances where the D.P. or director does not operate, the camera operator physically operates the camera. When multiple cameras are required, additional operators are used.

5/55 Camera Assistant: In prep, the A/C checks out the camera, making certain that it is working properly and that all the necessary accessories are included. On the shoot, the A/C loads and unloads magazines of film, follows focus, keeps the slate that identifies numbered takes, keeps camera reports (a written record of each take, by number, including footage counts and film stock used, which tells the lab which takes to process) and, in general, maintains the camera equipment. Frequently, the A/C has additional OT after the general crew wrap, which is time needed to pack the camera, and to 'can out' and pack the exposed film to go to the lab.

6/56 Outside Prop: Property people, in general, are responsible for procuring and maintaining the various 'furnishings' that make up the scene to be photographed. The outside prop meets with the director and set designer, surveys locations, and 'shops' for the necessary 'dressing'. He locates each item and purchases or rents furniture, fixtures, tableware, hand props, featured key props, and any item needed to create atmospheric effects (e.g. smoke, fog, rain, etc.)

8/58 Inside Prop: Sometimes known as 'set dresser', the inside props receive the items arranged for by outside props, unpack and inventory them, and place them on the set. Note: On a prelite day, when the sets have already been dressed and construction/dressing crews are no longer present, it is necessary to have inside props on the set to move props as needed, and to deal with any last-minute changes proposed by the agency or client when they visit the set. On the shoot, all props working on the shoot are, effectively, inside props. They handle all the props, keeping items that 'work' in the scene replenished and in good order. For car shoots they are responsible for keeping the cars clean and ready for photography at all times. Note: It is quite common for the 'outside' prop to move 'inside', once all shopping has been completed, and all the props acquired.

11/61 Electrician: The head electrician is also known as key gaffer. The electrician scouts the locations with the D.P. and the director, checks on available power, and assists the D.P. in placing equipment orders. He selects additional electricians to work with him (Note: In general, all department heads select their second, third, and fourth men and so forth...) as the job requires. He supervises the staff in his department and works closely with the D.P. to execute his instructions to give the desired effect. (Note: The D.P. usually has the option to select the key gaffer on a shoot.)

16/66 Grip: The key grip scouts the location if any rigging or special problems are anticipated. On the prelite he loads in the equipment, and sets up stands to support lights or any other hanging elements, sets up dollies and track, cranes, etc. On the shoot, the grip department operates the dolly and/or crane, moves any heavy equipment and loads in and out.

20/70 Mixer: The head person in the sound department. He selects the other members of his department, and is responsible for the overall quality of the sound. He decides the best means of each take to determine its quality.

21/71 Boom Man: Operates the microphone boom on each sound take.

22/72 Recordist: He acts as the mixer's assistant, keeping a written record of each numbered sound take, which is sent with the original ¼" tape to be transferred to magnetic stripe.

23/73 Playback: Operates the recording machine which plays back a pre-recorded track for each take, so that the actors or dancers can adjust the timing of their speech or movements to match that track.

24/74 Make-up: Applies make-up to all on-camera talent. Also supervises and/or manufactures any special prosthetics required. Note: Often will require assistance in order to have large numbers of talent ready at the same time.

25/75 Hair: Dresses the hair on all on-camera talent. Also supervises the fitting of any wigs or mustaches.

26/76 Stylist: Designs and supervises the construction and fitting of any special costumes. Selects clothing for all talent, renting or purchasing items as needed. Supervises wardrobe fittings. Contacts all talent in advance of the shoot, to check their sizes and advises them as to what personal clothing they should bring to the shoot. On the shoot, the stylist makes final wardrobe choices with the director and agency, and stands by on the set to make any adjustments. The stylist is responsible for details of wardrobe continuity for matching action.

27/77 Wardrobe Attendant: Asst. to the stylist. Organizes wardrobe in advance of the shoot when large numbers of talent are involved. Performs alterations, and maintains the wardrobe (pressing, hemming, etc.) on set. Packs the clothes when shooting is completed.

28/78 Script Supervisor: Keeps a detailed record (script notes) of the day's shooting. Is responsible for maintaining continuity so there are no problems matching scenes. Script notes are the official record of the shoot, and are sent with the dailies to the editor, to aid in postproduction.

29/79 Home Economist: Tests any food products to be photographed in advance of the shoot, to determine the best ways to prepare the product to make it look its best for photography. Shops for any foods needed on the shoot. On the set, prepares all food to be photographed.

30/80 Assistant Home Ec: See above. Washes dishes, peels potatoes, selects unbroken potato chips, etc... In general, assists the home ec.

31/81 VTR Operator: Operates the videotape recorder fed by the video assist unit (video tape) on the camera. His responsibility is to record and play back what the camera is recording during takes, for immediate review on set or location.

32/82 EFX Operator: Sets up and operates any equipment which provides a special effect (e.g. rain, smoke, wind, snow) or any special rigging required (e.g. harnesses and pulleys to 'fly' an actor).

33/83 Scenic: Applies wallpaper and paint on locations where extensive work of this sort is required. Paints special signs needed for dressing. Note: Scenic labor in the painting of sets, backdrops, cycs, etc. is included in set labor (Category G). On studio shoots of more than one day, a standby scenic is hired and would appear in Category B.

34/84 Teleprompter Operator: Operates equipment which displays the actors lines so that they can be prompted while the camera is rolling. Most often used in single take commercials, with celebrities, or with non-professional talent.

35/85 Generator Operator: Self-explanatory.

36/86 Still Photographer: Shoots production stills and publicity stills as requested.

37/87 Location Contact/Scout: Searches for locations per specs provided by the director. Researches and photographs all possibilities. Returns to select choices with the agency and director, and clears the final location, aids in securing all necessary permissions and making logistical arrangements for the shoot day. May be present on the shoot as well, if there is a complicated schedule involving many locations or a particular location that requires special handling.

38/88 P.A.: (usually several). General all-purpose production assistants who perform many and varied functions. May assist producer or director, do office clerical work, run out on last-minute errands, pickup and set up meals, answer phones and assist in any way necessary.

Appendix B (continued)

39/89 A.D.: Assistant to the first A.D. in preparing the shoot and running the set. Often responsible for putting out talent calls, and handling the talent on the set, signing actors in and out, and obtaining signed contracts from them. (Note: The DGA requires that companies hire a 2nd A.D. for at least one day of every shooting, and for all shoot days on any location shoot lasting four or more consecutive days.)

40/90 Nurse/First Aid: Hired to take care of any infants or very young children on set or location.

41/91 Craft Service: An optional union category on the West Coast, this person acts as a handyman on set, running errands and keeping the set clean and orderly and, in general assisting the prop, grip, and electric department.

42/92 Fire Fighter: Used frequently in California where permits often require a fireman standing by on location....sometimes with fire truck.

43/93 Police Officer: Sometimes required by law enforcement agencies if permit regulations call for police. Necessary as well on any exterior shooting where crowd control or traffic control are required. (Note: The City of NY will provide police assistance at no charge if their manpower needs allow.)

44/94 Welfare Teacher: Required where child labor laws mandate it.

45/95 Teamster: Drives all vehicles transporting equipment, props, cranes, and other elements of a production. Also needed to drive, or 'cover' any picture cars being photographed. (Note: Teamster requirements vary greatly depending on city where shoot takes place.)

CATEGORY "C"

101 Auto Rentals: All vehicles used for scouting and prepping location shoots. Includes long-term rentals (i.e. weekly) of production vehicles on out-of-town shoots.

102 Air Fares: Costs of air fares for all crew people traveling in pre-production only. (i.e. location scouting, director's scout, location surveys by prop, D.P. or whatever, casting trips, etc.)

103 Per Diems: Hotel and meal expenses for travel as above.

104 Still Camera & Film: Most often covers the cost of 35mm still cameras and film purchase and processing, used for scouting locations. Could also cover the rental of any special still equipment. (Note: Still equipment used for photographing during the production of the commercial should be listed in the equipment Category "I".)

105 Messengers: Messenger services used to transport paperwork and production materials to and from production company and agency, casting services, location services, equipment rental companies, editors, etc.

106 Trucking: Rental charges for all trucks used to transport the elements of production, e.g. props and equipment, on load and unload days only. The truck charges on the shoot days will appear in Category "D".

107 Deliveries & Taxis: Cabs to transport production personnel, e.g. to/from casting sessions, agency meetings, studios, in-town locations on prep days, etc. Also delivery charges from suppliers for pick-up and drop-off of various production requirements.

108 Home Ec. Supplies: Purchases of food to be photographed. Rental of refrigerators, stoves, and other equipment needed to prepare and store food for photography.

109 Telephone & Cable: Self-explanatory.

110 Casting: Charges by casting directors for their time spent in auditioning talent. Includes preparation time in researching and placing cast calls, as well as time spent actually taping sessions and callbacks. Also may include time spent researching and booking extras.

111 Casting Facilities: The rental of videotape casting studios and equipment to tape talent auditions. Also includes the cost of the videotapes, rental of Polaroid camera and film to Polaroid each actor, and costs to make duplicate tapes for shipment to agency/client for approvals.

112 Working Meals: The cost of sandwiches, etc. provided for production personnel who work through without taking regular meal breaks, due to the exigencies of production.

CATEGORY "D"

114 Location Fees: The amount charged by the location for the rental of the premises for photography. May also include a charge from the location services who has the 'listing' for that location. (Similar to a commission from a broker or agent)

115 Permits: Charges levied by the governing municipal authority in whose jurisdiction the location lies. (Not always easy in an estimate to determine in whose jurisdiction an unknown location may be....)

116 Car Rentals: Automobiles used to transport crew, talent and agency to a shoot.

117 Bus Rentals: Vehicles used to transport larger numbers of crew, talent and agency to location on the shoot day. May also cover rental of 15-passenger vans in lieu of buses, to facilitate split calls.

118 Camper/Dressing Room Vehicles: Needed to provide additional makeup/wardrobe/dressing room space as well as additional lavatories if provisions at the location are not adequate.

Appendix B (continued)

May also be used to provide shelter on cold exteriors. Mandatory in California for childrens' classrooms for schooling...must be a separate vehicle from crew/client vehicle.

119 Parking, Tolls, Gas: For all trucks and production vehicles. In California, may include crew mileage reimbursement, required for "drive to" locations.

120 Trucking: Rental of trucks to transport equipment to the shoot (on shoot days only. Load and unload rentals appear in Category "C").

121/122 Other Vehicles: Any other rented production vehicles. May be prop trucks, wardrobe vans, etc.

123 Customs: Charges incurred to itemize equipment, prepare paperwork and clear equipment and film through customs authorities on international shoots.

124 Air Freight/Excess Baggage: Overweight charges from the airlines for the transport of cases of equipment or other production elements, over the standard baggage allowance.

127/127 Air Fares: For travel of crew to a shoot on a distant location.

126/128 Per Diems: Hotel and meal expenses for above. (Note: There are two lines for each of the above two categories, to allow for the separate listing of different itineraries, or different legs of an extended shoot in multiple locations.)

129 Breakfast: Provided for crew, talent and agency on shoot. Can be the cost of the actual food, or meal monies that are contractually required for union crew members.

130 Lunch: See breakfast.

131 Dinner: See breakfast.

132 Guards: Hired for security where props, wardrobe or equipment are left overnight or out of doors at an unguarded location.

133 Limousines: To transport celebrity talent where requested.

134 Cabs and Other Transportation: Transportation of production personnel to and from shoot by means other than rented vehicles above.

135 Kit Rental: Fees paid to make-up, hair and other union crew members for the use of tools and supplies which they bring with them to the shoot.

136 Art Work: Special signs or props to dress a location.

137 Gratuities: Paid to contacts at locations; to maintain good will and ensure favorable cooperation. Also "tips" to bellboys, redcaps, etc.

CATEGORY "E"

140/141 Props: Rental and/or purchase of furniture, draperies, tableware, greenery, hand props—in short, all the various items needed to dress a location to make it look as desired, plus all the many miscellaneous behind-the-scenes items needed in support of this (i.e. ladders, nails, curtain rods, furniture blankets, tapes, sash cord, glue, hand tools, etc.) Note: For props to dress a set, see Category "H".

142/143 Wardrobe: Rental and purchase of clothing to dress all talent, including the cost of fabricating any special costumes.

144 Picture Vehicles: The rental of cars, taxis, carriages, trucks, busses, tractors, etc. to be photographed as part of the scene. Includes costs connected with researching and locating the appropriate vehicles, as well as the cost of transporting them to and from the shoot.

145 Animals and Handlers: Dogs, cats, horses or any other animals to be photographed,

accompanied by trainers/wranglers to care for the animals on the set, and hopefully to persuade them to do the required action repeatedly.

146 Wigs & Mustaches: Self-explanatory. (Most often used in "period" commercials)

147 Color-correction: Self-explanatory. Most often an agency/client responsibility.

CATEGORY "F"

STUDIO RENTAL: Studio Rental:

151 Build Days: Rental charged by studio on days when crew is constructing sets.

152 Build OT: Any OT for lengthier build days beyond the normal studio day.

153 Pre-lite Days: Rental charged by studio on days when sets are being lit.

154 Pre-lite OT: Studio OT for a longer than normal pre-lite would appear here.

155/156/157/158 Shoot Days, Shoot OT, Strike Days, Strike OT, as above.

159 Generator & Operator: More common on the West Coast, where studios often charge additional. Could also be charged in other areas on a very large lighting job where the studio's power is not sufficient.

160 Set Guards: Needed where very costly items are left overnight in a studio whose security is not sufficient.

161 Total Power Charge & Bulbs: It is customary in other areas for power charges to be billed by the studio on a per day or hour basis, with rates varying for build/strike, pre-lite and shoot. There is either a charge for power OT as well on longer shooting days. Bulb charges would appear here if they are included by the studio in their invoice, because they supplied the bulbs. In most cases, however, bulb charges would appear in the equipment Category ("I").

Appendix B (continued)

162 Miscellaneous Studio Charges: Includes coffee provided by the studio for the construction crew, rubbish removal, phone usage charges, and any other miscellaneous items not covered elsewhere in the estimate.

163 Meals: The cost of breakfast on the shoot day, as well as catered meals if the crew or talent are not broken, as well as meal monies where contractually required.

CATEGORY "G"

168 Set Designer/Art Director: Days spent by the set designer in attending meetings, doing set sketches and working drawings, ordering supplies, and supervising the construction and dressing of the sets.

169 Carpenters: Hired to fabricate construction materials in order to build a set.

170 Grips: Manpower hired to physically erect the sets, using the materials cut by the carpenters. These grips are employed for construction only; additional grips for pre-lighting the sets would appear in Category "A".

171 Outside Props: Man-days needed for one or more prop people to shop for the items needed to furnish and dress the sets. Note that, in a shoot that involved both sets and locations, the location shopping days would appear in Category "A". This category applies to sets only.

172 Inside Props: Additional props hired to receive, unload, inventory and unpack the props selected by the outside props, and to place them in the sets. (See note under Category "A" regarding additional props who may be required to standby on the pre-lite day, when the sets are already dressed.

173 Scenics: Hired to paint the sets, as well as backdrops and cycs as needed. They also apply wallpaper.

174 Electricians: Would appear on this line if the construction of the set requires a special electrical effect, or special wiring, or if it is necessary to hire an electrician to set up work lights for the construction crew. Labor to prelite the set is not set labor, and would appear in Category "A".

175 Teamsters: Drivers of trucks used to pick up set materials and props should properly be in this category.

176 Strike Crew: Men hired at the completion of photography to strike the lights and the sets, to load them onto a truck or otherwise dispose of them. Usually includes grips, props, electricians, and sometimes scenics to repaint a cyc, or carpenters to help dismantle an extensive set.

177 P.A'S: Hired to standby on the stage during construction and strike to keep paperwork organized, and to obtain any last-minute items needed by the construction crew.

CATEGORY "H"

181/182 Props, Rental and Purchase: Props obtained specifically for inclusion in a set, or hand-props which will be needed for scenes being shot in a set. On a job that is exclusively sets, there will be no props listed in Category "E". On a job which has both sets and locations, there will be costs in both categories. See Category "E" for an explanation of what 'props' entail.

183 Lumber: Materials ordered by set designer or carpenters, to be used to build the sets. This category does not include lumber used by the grip to support camera mounts or lights.

184 Paint: For painting sets or cycs. Also includes painting supplies like brushes, rollers, sprayers, cleaning materials, etc. Usually also includes wallpaper.

185 Hardware: Nails, clamps and etc. used to construct the set. May also include tool rentals, e.g. saws, nail guns, etc.

186 Special Effects: A miscellaneous category that might include smoke, fog, rain, lighting, special backdrops, extensive greenery, or any special effect.

187 Special Outside Construction: Any special prop or effect that is not built by the crews on the stage, but is provided by an independent supplier, e.g. a model-maker, who fabricates it, and then supplies it for the shoot. Also refers to set pieces that are built by an outside set service and then transported to the stage to be erected.

188 Trucking: The rental of vehicles used to transport set materials, props, and any special outside construction to and from the studio. Does not include transport of equipment. Note: Drivers for these vehicles should be listed on Line 175.

189 Messengers & Deliveries: Messenger services charges for the pick-up and delivery of paperwork and small items. Should apply to items connected with the set construction only, e.g. wallpaper samples, set sketches, etc.

190 Kit Rental: Money paid to scenics, prop department, etc. for the use of their supplies.

CATEGORY "I"

193 Camera Rental: All motion picture camera equipment may be described in detail when necessary, e.g. MOS, sound, high speed, etc.

194 Sound Rental: All audio recording equipment, microphones, booms, tape, etc.

195 Lighting Rental: Includes incandescent, HMI, and any special job needs. Also bulbs, gels and other diffusion materials.

196 Grip Rental: General purpose equipment used in conjunction with lighting sound, camera, etc. This includes dolly tracks, parallels, stands for lights, lumber, etc.

Appendix B (continued)

197 Generator Rental: Source of electrical energy sometimes needed both on location and in the studio. Small ones can be towed and large ones have their own vehicle. Needed to provide power to run camera, sound and lighting equipment.

198 Crane/Cherry Picker Rental: Wheeled vehicle that usually carries camera, camera man and director. Comes in many different types, and is used to facilitate camera moves or positions where elevated camera is desired.

199 VTR Rental: Video equipment which permits what is being photographed by the camera to appear on a monitor. Note: Can be used with or without playback feature.

200 Walkie Talkies/ Bull Horns: Used to communicate with members of the crew and cast on a large set, or on location where crew and cast may be dispersed over a large area.

201 Dolly Rental: A wheeled platform on which a camera is mounted. Used for both stationary and moving camera shots.

202 Camera Car: Specially outfitted vehicle upon which the camera is mounted. Mostly used for running shots on location.

203 Helicopter: Various types depending on job. Also includes special camera mount. Rental based on time aloft and distance flown from home base, as well as fuel support vehicles.

204 Production Supplies: Covers a very large miscellaneous category gels, rope, cards, tools, stands and most items often referred to as "expendables" which, once used cannot be re-used.

205 Teleprompter: Electronic means of assisting actors with the script. Usually mounted where the camera lens is, and controlled by teleprompter operator.

211 Purchase of Raw Stock/Footage Amount: Usage usually confined to 16mm or 35mm size. Comes in 400' or 1000' rolls.

212 Developing Footage Amount: Per foot charge by lab to develop the exposed negative.

213 Printing Footage Amount: Second step in processing is printing selected takes. This (positive) film is also called "dailies".

214 Transfer to Mag: Sound is recorded on ¼" tape, and then transferred to 16mm or 35mm sprocketed magnetic tape.

215 Sync/Screen Dailies: Magnetic tape "track" must be matched or synchronized with dailies in order to be able to screen. If there is no sound, there will only be a charge for screening.

CATEGORY "K"

217 Petty Cash: Miscellaneous costs that always occur. Covers those areas that spontaneously crop up on all productions.

218 Air Shipping/ Special Couriers: The shipping of production materials (e.g. casting tapes, set sketches) to agency/client for approval prior to shoot. The shipping of film out of town. The return of product, art work, props, wardrobe or any other agency/client request that necessitate this use.

219 Phones & Cables: Any post production costs in this category.

220 Accountable Cash Expenditures under $15.00: A cost plus reconciliation category. Used to include very small purchases for which there are receipts that don't fall into usual areas.

221 External Billing Costs. Computer Accounting: Cost based on a percentage of all direct labor costs. Required because of detailed information requested by agency/client.

222 Special Insurance: Covers other than usual liability insurance costs. e.g. valuable furs, jewels, unusual hazard, special props, antiques, etc.

CATEGORY "L"

227 Prep: The period of time devoted by the director specifically to the job. Includes meetings with agency and client, involvement in casting, scouting location/or supervising sets and rehearsals and doing new story boards and shooting boards.

228 Travel: Time to go to distant locations.

229 Shoot Days: Days on set or location actually directing commercial.

230 Post Production: When required to be involved in editing of commercial.

Appendix C
AICE Post-Production Cost Summary

Bid Date:	
Post Production Co.:	Agency:
Address:	Address:
Telephone:	Telephone:
Contact:	Client:
Editor:	Product:
Job #:	Agency Job #:
Production Co.:	Agency Producer:
Address:	Agency Business Manager:
Telephone:	Agency Creative Director:
Contact:	Agency Writer:
Director:	Agency Art Director:

COMMERCIAL IDENTIFICATION

Title: Length: Code #:

_____ _____ _____
_____ _____ _____
_____ _____ _____
_____ _____ _____
_____ _____ _____

SCHEDULE

Shooting Date:	
Dailies:	
Edit Dates:	
Due Date:	
Material Required:	

SUMMARY OF ESTIMATED POST PRODUCTION COSTS:

			ESTIMATE			ACTUAL
1000	Prep	Total A				
2000	Sound	Total B				
3000	Opticals	Total C				
4000	Laboratory	Total D				
5000	Videotape	Total E				
6000	Miscellaneous	Total F				
7000	Labor (when applicable)	Total G				
8100	SUB-TOTAL: DIRECT COST	SUB-TOTAL				
8200	Mark-up (%)					
8300	Labor	Total G				
8000	TOTAL	TOTAL				
9100	Sales Tax					
9000	GRAND TOTAL	GRAND TOTAL				

Comments:

Appendix C (continued)

1000	PREP			ESTIMATE			ACTUAL	*TAX
1010	Sync Dailies	(	Ft)					
1020	Screening Room	(	Hrs)					
1030	Code Dailies	(	Ft)					
1040	Stock Footage Search + Fee							
1050								
		SUB-TOTAL A						

2000	SOUND							
2010	Narration Recording	(	Hrs)					
2020	Dialogue Replacement	(	Hrs)					
2030	Library Music Search + Fee							
2040	Sound Effects							
2050	Transfers + Stock							
2060	Scratch Mix	(	Hrs)					
2070	Final Mix	(	Hrs)					
2080	Mixed Mag(s)	(#	)					
2090	Optical Tracks	(x16) (	x35)					
2100	Video Sound Transfers							
2110	Video Sound Mix	(	Hrs)					
2120	Video Sound Stock							
2130	Audio Relay/Retrack		Hrs)					
2140								
2150								
		SUB-TOTAL B						

3000	OPTICALS							
3010	Artwork							
3020	Projections	(#	)					
3030	Title Prep + Photography							
3040	Matte Prep + Photography							
3050	Color Stand Photography							
3060	Rotoscoping	(	Ft)					
3070	Interpositive	(	Ft)					
3080	Cynex/Wedges	☐ REG ☐ BI-PACK (#	)					
3090	Optical Testing							
3100	Pre-Opticals							
3110	Optical Negative/Effects	☐ 16 ☐ 35 ☐ CRI ☐ IP (#	)					
3120	Duping/Blow-ups	☐ 16 ☐ 35 ☐ CRI ☐ IP ☐ BU (	Ft)					
3130	Animation							
3140								
		SUB-TOTAL C						

4000	LABORATORY							
4010	Negative Prep/Conform							
4020	Negative Develop + Print	(	Ft)					
4030	Reprints	☐ 16 ☐ 35 (	Ft)					
4040	Reversal Dupes	☐ B/W ☐ Color						
4050	Optical Track Processing							
4060	Answer Print 35mm	(#	)					
4070	Answer Print 16mm	☐ Reduction ☐ Contact (#	)					
4080	35mm Protection/Duplication Element	☐ IP ☐ CRI (#	)					
4090	16mm Protection/Duplication Element	☐ IP ☐ CRI (#	)					
4100	Release Print 35mm	(#	)					
4110	Release Print 16mm	☐ Reduction ☐ Contact (#	)					
4120	Print Breakdown							
4130								
		SUB-TOTAL D						

Appendix C (continued)

5000	VIDEOTAPE		ESTIMATE			ACTUAL	*TAX
5010	Work Pix to Cassette (Incl. Stock)	(#)					
5020	Film to Tape w/Color Correction	(Hrs)					
5030	Additional Machines	(#)					
5040	Ultimatte	(Hrs)					
5050	Time Compression	(Hrs)					
5060	Tape to Tape w/Color Correction	(Hrs)					
5070	Tape to Tape Transfers						
5080	Visible Time Coded Cassette	(#)					
5090							
5100	Off-Line Edit	(Hrs)					
5110	Off-Line Cassette	(#)					
5120	Video Layout/EDL						
5130	On-Line Edit	(Hrs)					
5140	Additional Machines	(#)					
5150	Digital Effects Equipment	(Hrs)					
5160	Special Effects Equipment	(Hrs)					
5170	Electronic Graphics	(Hrs)					
5180	Character Generator	(Hrs)					
5190	Color Camera	(Hrs)					
5200	B/W Camera	Hrs)					
5210							
5220	Tape Stock + Reels						
5230	Generic Master	(#)					
5240	Edited Master	(#)					
5250	Protection Master/Printing Dupe	(#)					
5260	Dubs	(#)					
5270	Finished Cassettes	(#)					
5280	Tape to Film Transfer						
5290							
5300		SUB-TOTAL E					

6000	MISCELLANEOUS						
6010	Deliveries + Messengers						
6020	Shipping						
6030	Editorial Supplies						
6040	Long Distance Telephone						
6050	Working Meals in Facilities						
6060	Airfare						
6070	Per Diem	(Days)					
6080	Room/Equipment Rental	(Days)					
6090							
6100		SUB-TOTAL F					

7000	LABOR						
7010	Pre-Production	(Days) (Hrs)					
7020	Editor	(Days) (Hrs)					
7030	Editor Overtime	(Days) (Hrs)					
7040	Ass't Editor	(Days) (Hrs)					
7050	Ass't Editor Overtime	(Days) (Hrs)					
7060	Travel Time	(Days) (Hrs)					
7070	Payroll Taxes						
7080							
7090	Fee						
7100		SUB-TOTAL G					

PAGE 2

169

Appendix D
AICE Glossary

1000   <u>PREP</u>

1010   SYNC DAILIES
            THE SYNCHRONIZATION OF SOUND AND PICTURE--USUALLY
            DAILIES OR RUSHES.

1020   SCREENING ROOM
            ROOM USED TO EITHER VIEW FILM ON A LARGE SCREEN
            FORMAT OR SCREEN A VIDEOTAPE MASTER.

1030   CODE DAILIES
            PROCESS OF ADDING SYNCHRONIZED EDGE NUMBERS ON
            BOTH PICTURE AND MAGNETIC SOUND TRACK TO
            FACILITATE DIALOGUE EDITING.

1040   STOCK FOOTAGE SEARCH + FEE
            EXISTING FOOTAGE OF VARIOUS SUBJECTS AVAILABLE
            (USUALLY ON A NON EXCLUSIVE BASIS) FOR PURCHASE.
            COSTS ENTAIL LICENSE FEES, LAB COSTS AND SEARCH
            COSTS.

2000   <u>SOUND</u>

2010   NARRATION RECORDING
            THE RECORDING OF AN ANNOUNCER IN A SOUND STUDIO
            FACILITY.

2020   DIALOGUE REPLACEMENT
            THE RECORDING OF SYNCHRONOUS DIALOGUE FOR A SCENE
            WHERE THE ORIGINAL RECORDING WAS IMPAIRED (EITHER
            BY TECHNICAL OR LOCATION PROBLEMS) OR THE VOICE
            OF AN ACTOR NEEDS TO BE CHANGED.

2030   LIBRARY MUSIC SEARCH + FEE
            EXISTING MUSIC OF VARIOUS TYPES AVAILABLE
            (USUALLY ON A NON EXCLUSIVE BASIS) FOR PURCHASE.
            COSTS ENTAIL LICENSE FEES, TRANSFERS AND SEARCH
            COSTS.

2040   SOUND EFFECTS
            PRE-RECORDED SOUND EFFECTS AVAILABLE FOR PURCHASE.
            ENTAILS COST OF EFFECT, TRANSFER AND STOCK.

2050   TRANSFERS + STOCK
            THE TRANSFERRING OF SOUND FROM ONE FORMAT TO ANOTHER.

2060   SCRATCH MIX
            THE EQUALIZATION AND BALANCING OF THE VARIOUS
            PRELIMINARY TRACKS USED AT THE EDITING STAGE ONTO
            ONE MIXED TRACK FOR PRESENTATION.

2070   FINAL MIX
             THE EQUALIZATION AND BALANCING OF THE VARIOUS FINAL
             TRACKS ONTO ONE MIXED TRACK (USUALLY A 3 OR 4
             CHANNEL "FULL COAT MASTER").

2080   MIXED MAG
             A COPY OF THE FINAL MIXED TRACK ON MAGNETIC STOCK.

2090   OPTICAL TRACK
             A COPY OF THE FINAL MIXED TRACK ON OPTICAL TRACK
             NEGATIVE STOCK USED TO MAKE COMPOSITE PRINTS.

2100   VIDEO SOUND TRANSFERS
             AUDIO TRANSFERS MADE BEFORE AND AFTER A VIDEO
             SOUND MIX.

2110   VIDEO SOUND MIX
             THE EQUALIZATION AND BALANCING OF VARIOUS SOUND
             TRACKS OF A VIDEO PROGRAM, OFTEN ON MULTI-CHANNEL
             AUDIO TAPE.

2120   VIDEO SOUND STOCK
             VARIOUS AUDIO TAPES USED FOR VIDEO SOUND MIXING.

2130   AUDIO RELAY/RETRACK
             RERECORDING THE AUDIO TRACK OF A MASTER VIDEOTAPE.

3000   <u>OPTICALS</u>

3010   ARTWORK
             THE CREATION OF ARTWORK OR SETTING OF TYPE USED TO
             SHOOT ONTO FILM STOCK FOR INTEGRATION INTO THE FINAL
             FILM OR TO TRANSFER TO VIDEOTAPE FOR INTEGRATION
             INTO THE FINAL VTR EDIT.

3020   PROJECTION
             PRECISION ENLARGEMENT OF A FILM FRAME USED TO
             DESIGN SIZE AND PLACEMENT OF TITLES OR OTHER GRAPHIC
             ELEMENTS.

3030   TITLE PREP + PHOTOGRAPHY
             THE PREPARATION OF SET TYPE FOR PHOTOGRAPHY AND THE
             PHOTOGRAPHING OF IT ONTO HIGH CONTRAST FILM STOCK.

3040   MATTE PREP + PHOTOGRAPHY
             THE CREATION OF THE ELEMENTS NECESSARY FOR A MATTE
             AND THE PHOTOGRAPHING OF THEM ONTO HIGH CONTRAST
             FILM STOCK.

3050   COLOR STAND PHOTOGRAPHY
             THE PHOTOGRAPHING OF COLOR ARTWORK OR CHROMES ONTO
             COLOR FILM STOCK.

3060   ROTOSCOPING
THE CREATION OF A MATTE THAT MUST MATCH EXISTING
ACTION ON A FRAME BY FRAME BASIS.

3070   INTERPOSITIVE
AN INTERMEDIATE FILM STOCK USED TO CREATE A NEGATIVE
FROM A NEGATIVE (OR TO PROTECT A NEGATIVE).

3080   CYNEX/WEDGES
SHOWS THE RANGE OF COLOR OR DENSITY AVAILABLE FROM
ANY GIVEN FRAME OF A SCENE.

3090   OPTICAL TESTING
OPTICAL TESTING DONE AT THE EDITING STAGE TO EITHER
REFINE THE CHOREOGRAPHY OF A PARTICULAR FILM
EFFECT OR TO SHOW IT AT THE PRESENTATION STAGE.

3100   PRE-OPTICALS
OPTICAL EFFECTS THAT MUST BE ACCOMPLISHED IN MORE
THAN ONE STAGE.

3110   OPTICAL NEGATIVE/EFFECTS
A NEGATIVE MADE FROM THE ORIGINAL CAMERA NEGATIVE
(CRI) OR FROM AN INTERPOSITIVE MADE FROM THE OCN
INCORPORATING THE FINAL EDIT AND ALL DESIRED OPTICAL
EFFECTS AND TITLES.

3120   DUPING/BLOW-UPS
EITHER THE DUPLICATION OF A PARTICULAR FILM ELEMENT
OR THE ENLARGING OF IT.

3130   ANIMATION
FOR USE WHEN ANIMATION IS TO BE SUBCONTRACTED
THROUGH THE EDITOR.

4000   <u>LABORATORY</u>

4010   NEGATIVE PREP/CONFORM
CUTTING AND PREPARING SELECTED NEGATIVE SCENES.

4020   NEGATIVE DEVELOP + PRINT
DEVELOPING OF EXPOSED NEGATIVE AND MAKING A PRINT
FROM IT.

4030   REPRINTS
MAKING AN ADDITIONAL PRINT FROM A NEGATIVE.

4040   REVERSAL DUPES
MAKING A PRINT FROM A PRINT ON EITHER COLOR OR B/W
REVERSAL FILM STOCK.

4050   OPTICAL TRACK PROCESSING
DEVELOPING AN OPTICAL TRACK NEGATIVE.

Appendix D (continued)

4060   ANSWER PRINT 35MM
        THE FIRST 35MM PRINT MADE FROM THE OPTICAL NEGATIVE,
        A + B ROLLS, OR PRINTING DUPE IN WHICH SCENE TO
        SCENE COLOR AND DENSITY CORRECTIONS ARE MADE.

4070   ANSWER PRINT 16MM
        SAME AS ABOVE EXCEPT PRINT IS 16MM. THE SOURCE
        NEGATIVE HOWEVER CAN BE EITHER 35MM OR 16MM.

4080   35MM PROTECTION/DUPLICATION ELEMENT
        THIS ELEMENT IS MADE FROM THE OPTICAL NEGATIVE OR
        A + B ROLLS AND IS USED TO PRINT FROM IN ORDER TO
        PROTECT THE ORIGINAL PRINTING MATERIAL. IT CAN
        BE MADE VIA CRI (DIRECT NEG TO NEG) OR VIA INTER-
        POSITIVE (AND INTERNEGATIVE).

4090   16MM PROTECTION/DUPLICATION ELEMENT
        SAME AS ABOVE EXCEPT MADE IN 16MM.

4100   RELEASE PRINT 35MM
        PRINTS MADE FOR DISTRIBUTION OF FINAL FILM USUALLY
        FROM A PROTECTION/DUPLICATION ELEMENT.

4110   RELEASE PRINT 16MM
        SAME AS ABOVE IN A 16MM FORMAT FROM EITHER A 35MM OR
        16MM SOURCE.

4120   PRINT BREAKDOWN
        THE LABOR AND COST NECESSARY TO BREAK DOWN AND
        INDIVIDUALLY BOX AND LABEL A RELEASE PRINT ORDER.

5000   VIDEOTAPE

5010   WORK PICTURE TO CASSETTE
        TELECINE. AFTER COMPLETION OF FILM ROUGH CUTS,
        "ONE-LIGHT" OR "ROUGH" TRANSFERS ARE MADE FOR
        AGENCY AND CLIENT APPROVAL. TYPICALLY, THESE
        CHARGES INCLUDE CASSETTE STOCK CHARGES.

5020   FILM TO TAPE WITH COLOR CORRECTION
        TELECINE. MASTER QUALITY TRANSFERS OF ORIGINAL
        MATERIAL WITH COMPLETE SCENE-TO-SCENE COLOR
        CORRECTION, AND REPOSITIONS ALONG THE X (LEFT-
        RIGHT), Y (UP-DOWN), AND Z (BLOW UPS OR ZOOMS)
        AXES. CHARGES INCLUDE A SINGLE VIDEOTAPE RECORDER.

5030   ADDITIONAL RECORD MACHINES
        SIMULTANEOUS RECORDING OF TRANSFER MATERIAL FOR
        A + B ROLL EDITING, VIEWING, REFERENCE, OR OFF-LINE
        EDITING.

5040   ULTIMATTE
        REQUIRED FOR SPECIAL COLOR MATTE SCENE COMPOSITING.

Appendix D (continued)

5050   TIME COMPRESSION
USE OF DEVICES WHICH ALLOW VARIABLE SPEED (HENCE,
VARIABLE TIME) TRANSFERS, TYPICALLY WITH AUDIO PITCH
COMPENSATION.

5060   TAPE TO TAPE WITH COLOR CORRECTION
RERECORDING OF MASTER GRADE VIDEOTAPES WITH SCENE-
TO-SCENE COLOR CORRECTIONS, A PROCESS SIMILAR TO
FILM TO TAPE TRANSFERS.

5070   TAPE TO TAPE TRANSFERS
ANY RERECORDING OF ORIGINAL VIDEOTAPE MATERIALS,
WHEN ADDITIONAL OR DIFFERENT FORMAT TAPES ARE
REQUIRED.

5080   VISIBLE TIME CODED CASSETTE
OFTEN REQUIRED FOR REFERENCE, OFF-LINE EDITING, AND
FOR MUSIC OR NARRATION RECORDING SESSIONS.

5100   OFF-LINE EDIT
SMALL FORMAT, GENERALLY NOT-FOR-AIR EDITING,
TYPICALLY USED FOR MAKING EDITING DECISIONS PRIOR
TO THE "ON-LINE" OR MASTER ASSEMBLY SESSION, AS
WELL AS FOR VARIOUS TYPES OF PRESENTATIONS. THIS
IS ANALAGOUS TO EDITING A FILM WORK PICTURE PRIOR
TO SHOOTING AN OPTICAL.

5110   OFF-LINE CASSETTE
VIDEOTAPE STOCK USED IN OFF-LINE EDITING.

5120   VIDEO LAYOUT/EDL
PREPARATION OF AN EDIT DECISION LIST
PRIOR TO AN ON-LINE EDITING SESSION.

5130   ON-LINE EDIT
LARGE FORMAT, MASTER VIDEOTAPE ASSEMBLY FOR
BROADCAST.

5140   ADDITIONAL MACHINES
ADDITIONAL AUDIO AND VIDEOTAPE MACHINES EMPLOYED
WHEN MULTIPLE SOURCES (FOR DISSOLVES, WIPES AND SOME
SPECIAL EFFECTS), OR WHEN SIMULTANEOUS EDITED
RECORDINGS ARE REQUIRED.

5150   DIGITAL EFFECTS EQUIPMENT
ANY OF A VARIETY OF DEVICES TYPICALLY USED DURING
THE EDIT SESSION FOR FREEZE FRAMES, BLOWUPS, AND
MANY TYPES OF SCENE TRANSITIONS.

5160   SPECIAL EFFECTS EQUIPMENT
OTHER DEVICES USED FOR CREATING SPECIAL VISUAL
EFFECTS.

5170   ELECTRONIC GRAPHICS
DEVICES WHICH ALLOW THE CREATION AND MANIPULATION
OF DIVERSE GRAPHICAL IMAGES, INCLUDING "PAINTING"
AND ANIMATION.

Appendix D (continued)

5180   CHARACTER GENERATOR
           DEVICES WHICH PRODUCE AND INSERT TEXT INTO THE
           PICTURE.

5190   COLOR CAMERA
           USED AS A SOURCE FOR LIVE ACTION, OR OTHER MULTI-
           COLOR ORIGINAL MATERIALS.

5200   BLACK + WHITE CAMERA
           USED AS A SOURCE FOR VARIOUS ORIGINAL SCENES OR
           ELEMENTS, TYPICALLY FOR TITLES AND "SUPERS".

5220   TAPE STOCK + REELS
           VIDEOTAPE STOCK, REELS AND BOXES USED IN VIDEOTAPE
           TRANSFERS AND EDITING.

5230   GENERIC MASTER
           VIDEOTAPE EDITED MASTER COMPLETE EXCEPT FOR
           "SUPERS", LOGOS, OR AUDIO TRACKS WHERE DIFFERENT
           VERSIONS ARE ANTICIPATED. TYPICALLY, THIS MASTER
           IS USED AS A PLAYBACK SOURCE IN THE CREATION OF
           AN "EDITED MASTER".

5240   EDITED MASTER
           COMPLETED VIDEOTAPE MATERIAL WHICH HAS BEEN EDITED
           WITH TEST BARS, SLATE AND TONE READY FOR AIR.

5250   SAFETY MASTER/PRINTING DUPE
           A COPY OF THE EDITED MASTER WITH IDENTICAL TIME
           CODE FROM WHICH DUBS ARE MADE.

5260   DUBS
           DUPLICATE COPIES OF A VIDEOTAPE.

5270   FINISHED CASSETTES
           CASSETTE COPIES OF FINISHED MASTERS.

5280   TAPE TO FILM TRANSFER
           FILM NEGATIVES AND PRINTS MADE FROM A VIDEOTAPE
           ORIGINAL.

6000   <u>MISCELLANEOUS</u>

6010   DELIVERIES + MESSENGERS
           LOCAL DELIVERIES OR MESSENGER SERVICES DIRECTLY
           RELATED TO A SPECIFIC JOB.

6020   SHIPPING
           SHIPPING OF ANY PRODUCTION MATERIAL LOCALLY OR LONG
           DISTANCE DIRECTLY RELATED TO A SPECIFIC JOB.

6030   EDITORIAL SUPPLIES
            PICTURE AND SOUND ACADEMY LEADERS, RAW STOCK FOR
           FILL, REELS, CANS, BOXES, CARTONS, SPLICING TAPE
           AND OTHER FILM SUPPLIES REQUIRED TO DO A SPECIFIC
           JOB (NOT ADHESIVE TAPE, PAPER CLIPS OR ITEMS THAT
           ARE NORMALLY CONSIDERED GENERAL OVERHEAD COSTS).

Appendix D (continued)

6040   LONG DISTANCE TELEPHONE
        LONG DISTANCE TELEPHONE CHARGES INCURRED DIRECTLY
        RELATED TO A SPECIFIC JOB.

6050   WORKING MEALS IN FACILITIES
        MEALS REQUESTED BY AGENCY REPRESENTATIVES WHEN
        WORK EXTENDS THROUGH THE MEALTIME PERIOD. THIS
        DOES NOT INCLUDE MEALS ORDERED IN FOR THE EDITOR
        ONLY, OR MEALS THAT ARE OFF THE PREMISES, FOR
        EXAMPLE BUSINESS LUNCHES OR DINNERS IN A LOCAL
        RESTAURANT.

6060   AIRFARE
        AIRLINE COSTS WHEN IT IS NECESSARY FOR AN EDITOR
        TO TRAVEL.

6070   PER DIEM
        AN ALLOWANCE FOR DAILY EXPENSES WHEN THE EDITOR
        AND/OR ASSISTANT IS ON LOCATION.

6080   ROOM/EQUIPMENT RENTAL
        RENTAL OF AN EDITING ROOM AND/OR EQUIPMENT WHEN
        IT IS NECESSARY FOR THE EDITOR TO TRAVEL TO
        LOCATION TO EDIT.

7000   LABOR

7010   PRE-PRODUCTION
        A FEE FOR THE TIME SPENT BY THE EDITOR IN THE
        PRE-PRODUCTION STAGE OF A SPECIFIC JOB.

7020   EDITOR
        THE HOURLY OR DAILY LABOR RATE FOR THE SERVICES
        OF THE EDITOR.

7030   EDITOR OVERTIME
        THE HOURLY OR DAILY LABOR RATE WHEN THE EDITOR IS
        REQUIRED TO WORK WEEKENDS, HOLIDAYS, OR AFTER
        NORMAL WORK TIMES.

7040   ASSISTANT EDITOR
        THE HOURLY OR DAILY RATE FOR ASSISTANT EDITORIAL
        SERVICES.

7050   ASSISTANT EDITOR OVERTIME
        THE HOURLY OR DAILY LABOR RATE WHEN AN ASSISTANT
        EDITOR IS REQUIRED TO WORK WEEKENDS, HOLIDAYS, OR
        AFTER NORMAL WORK TIMES.

7060   TRAVEL TIME
        TRAVEL TIME CHARGES FOR TRAVELING OUT OF THE CITY
        FOR AN EDITING SESSION.

7070   PAYROLL TAXES
        THIS LINE TO BE UTILIZED BY THOSE CITIES REQUIRING
        SPECIFIC BREAKOUT.

7090   FEE
        A CHARGE FOR AN ADDITIONAL CREATIVE OR SUPERVISORY
        SERVICE.

Appendix E
The Three-Legged Stool: An Advertiser Looks at Cost Control

For the next twenty-five minutes, the subject is cost controls in television commercial production. For those of you who are truly interested in this subject, twenty-five minutes is barely adequate. For those of you who are not at all interested in this subject, twenty-five minutes is barely endurable.

All of you will be relieved to know I am not going to talk about inflation, cable and satellite transmission or the new videodisc hardware. Nor will I address one of the major concerns of our industry today: What is Bert Parks doing now?

What I do have for you are some fresh ideas on the subject of television production costs, specifically, how to make cost controls an agency responsibility and how to make cost controls part of the creative process.

For those of you who may be considering an in-house production team at your company, I will give you an honest look at what can be achieved and an honest look at some of the problems you may encounter along the way.

To begin, I think we clients must recognize that some of our concepts about television production are outdated, outmoded and frequently counterproductive.

I am speaking specifically of the idea that cost controls can be effectively exercised at the bidding stage of the advertising, where most of us usually think the company production team begins. In my experience, this is simply too late. Cost controls exerted at this point are largely ineffectual. Worse, the company production team is already out of the mainstream of the advertising process and in the vulnerable position of coming in with too little, too late. This kind of late involvement almost always creates an adversary relationship—with the company producer, an adversary first of the agency and then, unwittingly, an adversary of brand and division management.

The notion of the company producer as the green eyeshade guy called in at the last minute to keep the agency honest or to get the fat out of the bid is as outdated as shooting your advertising in black and white. You have only to look at your agency structure to see what I mean. The old-line producer is gone. This was the experienced and seasoned pro who largely called the shots—who took the board from the hands of the writer and eliminated costly production elements by asking for a rewrite or who himself restaged the action. He's gone. These days, the line producer's function has been absorbed into the creative group. Now it's the writer or art director or creative director who importantly determines the production specifications: who should shoot the commercial, how many days of shooting, studio or location. These decisions largely influence the ultimate cost to you, the advertiser, and they are no longer considered production decisions, they are considered to be creative decisions. And since creative decisions have always been discussed with division management, where does the company producer fit in? He doesn't. He has no effective counterpart.

I think it is fair to say that if the agency has restructured its thinking, it is time for you, the client, to do the same—to rethink the entire advertising process and the role of the company producer if you have one or you're considering one. Rather than sending him in at the end of the decision-making process, he needs to go in up front. That's where truly effective, cost controls are generated—with the creative group: what they need, what they ask for, what they can't have. This is genuine cost control in today's world, or perhaps better said, genuinely effective management of your advertising dollars.

Are we considered tough to work with? You bet. And yet on the other side of it, how many of you receive letters from your agencies thanking you for your contribution to the advertising? That happens quite often at Gillette, and that's always a pleasant surprise and very gratifying.

Now before you rush out and decide you must have a system in place by next Friday, let me tell you that none of this has happened easily. Our system requires that both the divisions and the agencies agree to participate and cooperate fully. Our system requires a recognition that our department must be free to work with many groups inside the agency—account, creative, production, financial, media. In this sense, we have no agency counterpart. Some of our agency friends found that a little unsettling at first.

What is required to start up an advertising system inside a major company? The requirements are time, money and a willingness to change, and perhaps most important, the open and clearly stated support of senior company management. Fortunately at Gillette I had the support of two guys named Ryan. If you know Boston, believe me, it helps to have a couple of Irishmen on your team.

After top management support, you need the support of your operating divisions. They let our agencies know they wanted our systems and wanted them to be used. Let me stress that without this kind of strong division support, there is very little chance a new advertising group will have the opportunity to become established and mature.

The title of my talk today is "The Three-Legged Stool." This phrase originated with Bill Ryan, and it grew out of a memo sent around to our agencies to describe how he saw us all working together. Let me read you just a bit of what he wrote: "The best advertising originates if we recognize that the division, its agencies and advertising service are three legs of the same stool . . . each offering support, strength and balance as part of the marketing, creative and production process."

How does the three-legged stool concept work? When do we provide that support, strength and balance? Well, let me take you through the highlights of our system so you can see for yourself.

Our activities begin at the very beginning, in August of the year preceding the start of advertising. We work with the brand groups and their agencies to discuss all aspects of the advertising picture—television, radio, print, test advertising, full-finished advertising, promotion, talent and residual costs, commercial scheduling, media. We develop a dollars-and-cents forecast for the year and give this information to the brand groups. It is their responsibility to obtain formal division approval. Once we have it and the year begins, all approvals for advertising dollars must go through us. And once underway, each month we oversee the actual dollar flow and report these activities to each brand.

Why do *we* develop the spending plans for the year? Simply because experience has shown we are more accurate than either the brand groups or the agencies in generating reliable dollar forecasts. Under our system, we are able to control all aspects of spending, set ceilings in all categories and work with the agencies to achieve advertising created, produced and aired within those dollar guidelines. Under this system, no brand needs to pull dollars from print to TV to accommodate some dollar shortfall in the last quarter. They know month by month how they are doing.

The second highlight of our system is this—what we call the project initiation form. It's a timetable. We found through experience that it takes just about eight weeks to get copy written, rewritten and approved and about eight weeks to cast, bid, shoot, edit and clear the as-shot commercial through the networks. So simply by knowing when a brand wants to be on air, the agency knows when they have to get started.

If a snag develops along the line, we can both revise the production schedule and push the test of air date back to accommodate the time lost. This document looks simple. It is. But it has proved to be one of the most effective cost controls at our disposal because it gives the agency the opportunity to work in an open, productive manner and the brand group the time to fix and rework and tinker and, yes, even change its mind.

Let me talk for a moment about our relationship with the brand groups and the agencies in the creative process. There was a good deal of opposition to Advertising Services' becoming intimately involved with the creative aspects of the advertising. Brand groups feared we would represent another level of copy approval. Agencies feared we would somehow exercise our capabilities to stop advertising we thought too expensive.

We did neither, by design. We are now recognized to be creative advisors working with the agencies in the service of the brand groups. We encourage them to test whenever necessary, and we get our agencies the dollars they need for experimental shooting days. Our goal in all this is a simple one: We want to encourage and stimulate the agencies' visual thinking because, as you know, it isn't what you say as much as what you show that means really great advertising. We also want to alert both the agencies and the brand groups to any potential problems we see at the storyboard stage.

Let's face it: When you have helped create some 3,000 commercials, you have a pretty good feel for what works and what doesn't—how the copy is going to translate into a piece of effective film. In my experience, most so-called production problems are really copy problems that are only first recognized in the screening room. By working them out at the copy stage, we have helped play a significant role in speeding advertising along and eliminating scrapping.

We also give the brand groups some specific information about the advertising they are considering for production. We give them a probable cost to produce and a probable cost to air. Again, we are not trying to pick the advertising, that decision must be made by the divisions. But that decision must be based on solid, reliable information because, really, it is not just what a commercial costs that is important, the real consideration must be, "Is the commercial worth what it will cost to shoot?" Maybe this advertising is just transitional to get the brand on to a new campaign in the fall. If that's where they want to put the main thrust of their dollars, we've got to make sure they have the dollars available to spend then. What if the agency disagrees with our estimated cost of production? Well, we base our projected costs on the agency's track record: the director they usually go for, the number of shooting days they usually request. If the creative group says they really want to do this advertising and it will not cost what Advertising Services has indicated, the agency is now committed to bringing the advertising in at the figure *they* have suggested, and we believe they should be held to it.

Again, this is not an antagonistic attitude, no we versus them. It is a simple recognition that we expect sound, predictable outcomes. Someone once said that Advertising Services' banner should read, "No Surprises!" They have heard us say that so often. Well, I'll agree with that. I think in the advertising business, no surprises is a pretty good standard to carry forward.

By now I think it should be obvious that we believe the key to successful advertising happens a long time before any cameras turn. Getting everything right up front is key to effective dollar management.

When we move forward toward the actual production phase, we use the pre-production agenda form. This document asks the agency to put down in writing every production consideration up front. That's right. No surprises. All of this is done in advance of bidding or casting. This is our blueprint for the entire shooting. The production agenda must be specific, detailed and complete.

This working plan is prepared by the entire agency team—creative, production, account group—and it is reviewed by the entire company team—brand group, division management, Advertising Services. If anyone questions or disagrees or feels uneasy about something, we talk to the agency, and we rework that description or goal on paper.

If you don't have some sort of document like this inside your company, I think it is imperative you invent one because getting specific, getting your concerns out at this stage, on paper and changing your mind or the agency's, on paper, is a great deal more constructive and a great deal cheaper than trying to come to some consensus in the screening room after the film has been shot. Once again, if we agree in writing up front what we're after, we are once again committed to work together. We are a team.

This pre-production agenda serves as the spine of our pre-production activities, the thrust of our pre-production meeting, and later serves as the call report of the meeting, all generated before the fact. By using this, not only have you eliminated the chances for scrapping, you have also given the production company specifics: hard, detailed information that will lower your production costs 10 to 20 percent, before a camera ever turns. Why? Because the production company is assured you know what you want. Let's face it; production companies have been burned by indecisive clients in the past. If they smell indecision, they are going to cover themselves and pad the bid. So would I. So would you.

If you have a production team on staff, you can save even more at the bidding stage. We ask our agencies to discuss the production specifications with us before they go out for bids. Routinely, we help the agency rework their specs, we make small changes, scale down relatively minor elements and in the process often save a full day of production. This translates into a savings of about $35,000 up front. We also use the competitive three-bid system, the AICP form, and we examine all categories of expense thoroughly.

I would advise you not to use the cost-plus system unless you have a fully staffed in-house production group. Cost plus without thorough after-the-fact scrutiny is like giving the production house your credit card and asking them to send it back when they've bought all they need.

One other cost savings principle is putting a ceiling on editorial costs. Agencies tend to cut the film in successive waves—first the producer, then the writer, then the art director, then the creative director, and then maybe you, the client, ask, "Can I see it a couple of different ways?" Sure you can. But you've just added another $10,000 to $15,000 on that job. Don't do it. Put a flat ceiling on editorial, and have everything else, including any special opticals, to be approved as a special overage.

Do our agencies object to all this homework, before, during and after the shooting? Sure, It's hard work. But let me tell you, this system has been in place now for seven years. A number of our agencies have asked if they could use our system in dealing with their other clients. That says the system is working, for the agencies as well as the client.

You know, in any given year, my associate Jack Walp and I have to work through the conception, development, costs and shooting of about eighty commercials. We have the good experience and help of June Zeiner, our business affairs manager, who fortunately knows a lot about print and talent residuals.

Still and all, eighty commercials is a lot of work. We go to only about 60 percent of the shootings, where we can really contribute—where there's some difficult demonstration or a new product launch or there's some sensitive legal issue. But by and large, we leave it to the agencies to request our presence because, in our opinion, the agency has a lot of good people who really don't need us looking over their shoulders. They know what we want. We've told them. And we have confidence in their abilities to bring back a first-rate job.

Quite a number of creative directors and heads of production at our agencies have talked about this relationship. They tell us it feels good when the client trusts them. They use words like *professional, understanding, stimulating, supportive.* I think if you can generate those kinds of emotions inside your agencies, you are doing the job right.

For those of you who are the client out there today, let me remind you that you have the ability to truly control costs by what you demand and what you give to your agencies. When you create an atmosphere of trust and openness, when you encourage your agencies to do their best work and give them time to work, you have done it. You have made cost controls an inherent outgrowth of the creative process.

Index

About the Author

RON HARDING is President of Harding & Company, a consulting firm specializing in advertising and communications. He was Director of Advertising Production for Gillette for thirteen years and Production Supervisor at Procter & Gamble for nine years. His articles have appeared in *Advertising Age*, *Backstage*, and *Business Week*.